THE

KITCHEN PANTRY
SCIENTIST

ECOLOGY
FOR KIDS

THE
KITCHEN PANTRY
SCIENTIST

ECOLOGY
FOR KIDS

Science **EXPERIMENTS AND ACTIVITIES** Inspired
by **AWESOME ECOLOGISTS**, Past and Present

LIZ LEE HEINECKE

QUARRY

Inspiring | Educating | Creating | Entertaining

First Published in 2023 by Quarry Books, an imprint of The Quarto Group,
100 Cummings Center, Suite 265-D, Beverly, MA 01915, USA.
T (978) 282-9590 F (978) 283-2742 Quarto.com

Quarry Books titles are also available at discount for retail, wholesale, promotional, and bulk purchase. For details, contact the Special Sales Manager by email at specialsales@quarto.com or by mail at The Quarto Group, Attn: Special Sales Manager, 100 Cummings Center, Suite 265-D, Beverly, MA 01915, USA.

10 9 8 7 6 5 4 3 2 1

ISBN: 978-0-7603-7569-3

Digital edition published in 2023
eISBN: 978-0-7603-7570-9

Library of Congress Cataloging-in-Publication Data

Names: Heinecke, Liz Lee, author.
Title: Ecology for kids : science experiments and activities inspired by
    awesome ecologists, past and present / Liz Lee Heinecke.
Description: Beverly, MA : Quarry Books, an imprint of The Quarto Group,
    2023. | Series: Kitchen Pantry scientist | Includes index. | Audience:
    Ages 7-10 | Audience: Grades 2-3 | Summary: "The Kitchen Pantry
    Scientist : Ecology for Kids features biographies of 25 leading
    ecologists, past and present, accompanied by accessible and engaging
    experiments and activities to bring the history and principles of
    ecology alive"-- Provided by publisher.
Identifiers: LCCN 2022040541 (print) | LCCN 2022040542 (ebook) | ISBN
    9780760375693 (trade paperback) | ISBN 9780760375709 (ebook)
Subjects: LCSH: Ecologists--Biography--Juvenile literature. |
    Ecology--Experiments--Juvenile literature.
Classification: LCC QH26 .H45 2023 (print) | LCC QH26 (ebook) | DDC
    577--dc23/eng/20220921
LC record available at https://lccn.loc.gov/2022040541
LC ebook record available at https://lccn.loc.gov/2022040542

Series Design: Debbie Berne
Cover Illustrations: Kelly Anne Dalton/Lilla Rogers Studio
Cover Photography: Amber Procaccini Photography
Illustration of Author: Mattie Wells (cover and page 3)
Design and Page Layout: Megan Jones Design
Photography: Amber Procaccini Photography
Illustration: Kelly Anne Dalton/Lilla Rogers Studio

Printed in Singapore

"All things are one thing and that one thing is all things—plankton, a shimmering phosphorescence on the sea and the spinning planets and an expanding universe, all bound together by the elastic string of time. It is advisable to look from the tide pool to the stars and then back to the tide pool again."

—JOHN STEINBECK

CONTENTS

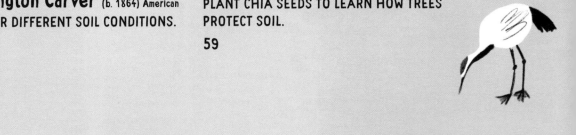

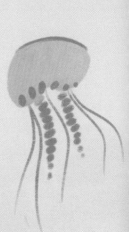

INTRODUCTION

> "The word *ecology* simply comes from the Greek word meaning 'house,' so it symbolizes our total house, our total environment. And that's what ecology is. It is a study of, an understanding and preservation of, the total environmental picture."
> —EUGENE ODUM

Life on Earth is a balancing act that depends on the interactions between living organisms and their physical environments. An ecosystem is an area where microbes, plants, and animals fight to claim space and work together to form a pocket of life, often depending on each other for survival. Ecosystems can be big or small, located in a rotting log or along a rocky shoreline. Regardless, they are fascinating reflections of how life on Earth evolved to cover every square inch with organisms best suited to survive in certain environments.

Ecology is defined as the study of how living organisms interact with each other and their physical environments. *The Kitchen Pantry Scientist: Ecology for Kids* introduces readers to twenty-five inspiring scientists whose work is related to ecology. Because exploration,

observation, and experimentation bring science to life, this book gives kids the opportunity to explore a number of fascinating ecosystems on the page and then explore them further using hands-on projects.

While modern ecology has only been around since the 1800s, humans have been observing living things in their natural environments since they first walked the Earth. We know from cave paintings that early humans watched animals and understood that they often moved in herds. Indigenous peoples were the first ecologists. Their survival depended on using traditional ecological knowledge passed down for generations to maintain the healthy, diverse ecosystems that sustained them.

In the fourth century, the Greek philosopher Aristotle and his student Theophrastus described plants and animals, along with their relationships with the environment. Then, in the nineteenth century, Charles Darwin famously studied how environmental pressures affected plants and animals in the Galápagos Islands. Those observations eventually led him to propose his important theory of evolution.

For a long time, the field of ecology was dominated by European and American men, but this book demonstrates how that has changed. We begin in the eighteenth century, with the story of Alexander von Humboldt, a famous German explorer who went on fantastic adventures and made countless important discoveries. After learning about von Humboldt, readers can try a hands-on project to see how cold water rises from the ocean floor to create nutrient-rich currents that feed millions of animals. In another lab, kids build their own tide pool in a bin, adding and removing water to see how intertidal communities are affected by waves and water.

Well-known ecologists and biologists such as William Emerson Ritter, George Washington Carver, G. Evelyn Hutchinson, Rachel Carson, and Wangari

Maathai are all featured. The book is written in chrono-logical order and features several inspiring contemporary biologists from around the world. After reading about fish biologist Lesley de Souza, readers can build a rain forest terrarium or an aquatic ecosystem. Ayana Elizabeth Johnson's lab involves using carbonated water to see how excess carbon dioxide is making oceans more acidic.

Ecology for Kids will introduce readers to many fascinating people and ecosystems. It is a good reminder that we are all part of a much larger ecosystem called Earth. I hope this book inspires readers to understand that although animals compete, they must also cooperate to protect the delicate balance that sustains life.

"There are opportunities even in the most difficult moments."
—WANGARI MAATHAI

LAB 1

Alexander von Humboldt

(b. 1769)

A CURIOUS MIND

Born in Prussia, which later became Germany, Alexander von Humboldt would grow up to be a famous geographer, geologist, naturalist, and explorer. From the time he was young, he loved to collect and identify plants, animals, and shells, and he never lost his curiosity about the natural world. His tutor, Carl Ludwig Willdenow, taught him to pay attention to where different types of plants grew, a lesson that Alexander never forgot. He studied economics, geology, anatomy, astronomy, and languages before going to work at a gold mine, where he was as interested in the plants on the surface as the minerals beneath the ground. Longing to see the world, he went to explore the Spanish colonies of the Americas with botanist and physician Aimé Bonpland.

AN EXPLORER

In Venezuela, they climbed a volcano, explored caves, and met local peoples. Alexander noted that a lake was evaporating because the trees around it had been cut down, which was an early description of climate change caused by humans. Alexander was thrilled when the Indigenous people helped him catch some electric eels but didn't realize that they carried a deadly electrical charge for several hours after they died. He was badly shocked while dissecting one of them.

MOUNTAINS AND PLANETS

Landing in Cuba, he and Bonpland aided a Scottish botanist and his son who had been shipwrecked there. They collected and preserved trunks full of plants and animals and did a survey of minerals in the country. They climbed a mountain and made it to 19,286 feet (5,878 m), a world record for Westerners at that time. In Peru, they watched the planet Mercury pass across the sun and Alexander studied the potential of bird and bat droppings (guano) as fertilizer for plants.

A 4,000-PAGE DIARY

Alexander and his traveling companion then went to Mexico, which was called "New Spain." In Mexico, he visited silver mines and continued to study plants, animals, and geology. He was extremely interested in the country's ancient civilizations and the Incan ruins he saw there. Stopping in the United States, Alexander met with President Thomas Jefferson, who was interested to learn that Alexander had discovered mammoth teeth near the equator during his travels. When he returned to Germany, his diary from the trip (1799–1804) was about 4,000 pages long.

CHAIN OF CONNECTION

Alexander's observations allowed him to recognize the relationship between all living things and their physical environment. He saw that biology, the atmosphere, the ocean, and the earth are all intertwined. In his work *Cosmo*, Alexander wrote, "In considering the study of physical phenomena, we find its noblest and most important result to be a knowledge of the chain of connection, by which all natural forces are linked together, and made mutually dependent on each other." Alexander inspired many scientists, artists, writers, and naturalists, including Charles Darwin, who later proposed the theory of evolution by natural selection.

IN TODAY'S WORLD

One of Alexander Von Humboldt's greatest achievements was sharing what he learned on his expeditions with the public and other scientists, using lectures, maps, and drawing. Today, it is more important than ever that scientists communicate well with the public, as we face enormous challenges such as climate change and pandemics.

COLD CURRENTS

Use blue ice cubes and water to see how wind brings cold ocean currents to the surface.

MATERIALS

- Water
- Blue food coloring
- Ice cube tray
- Rocks of various sizes
- Clear container such as a deep casserole dish or a large plastic container
- Old sock or piece of cheesecloth
- Twist tie
- Scissors
- Drinking straws

SAFETY TIPS AND HINTS

Supervise small children around containers filled with water.

Wear gloves when handling blue ice cubes to avoid staining your hands.

PROTOCOL

1 Mix water and blue food coloring together to make dark blue water. Pour into the ice cube tray. Freeze. *Fig. I*

2 Place several rocks in the container, leaving the center clear. Fill the container with lukewarm water. *Fig. 2*

3 Fill the toe of an old sock with five or six blue ice cubes and tie it tightly with a produce bag tie, and then cut off the extra cloth. *Fig. 3*

4 Put the sock of blue ice cubes in the center of the container to represent cold water at the bottom of the ocean. Weight it down by placing a rock on top of it. *Fig. 4*

5 From the side of the container, observe what happens to the cold blue water from the ice cubes as they melt. Cold water is denser (heavier) than warm water. *Fig. 5*

6 When there is a layer of ice-cold blue water on the bottom of the container, use a straw to blow air across the surface of the water in one direction, as if it were wind on the ocean. *Fig. 6*

7 Observe what happens to the cold blue water. Where does it rise to the surface? *Fig. 7*

8 Use a straw to blow "wind" on the water from another direction and observe the motion of the cold water.

Fig. 7: Observe what happens to the cold blue water.

Fig. I: Mix water and blue food coloring to make ice cubes.

CREATIVE ENRICHMENT

Repeat the experiment, but this time add 2 tablespoons (30 g) of salt per 4 cups (960 ml) of water in the container to represent the salinity (saltiness) of sea water. Does this change anything?

Fig. 2: Arrange rocks in a container and fill it with lukewarm water.

Fig. 3: Put several blue ice cubes in a sock and tie it tightly.

Fig. 4: Place the sock in the center of the container and weigh it down.

Fig. 5: The blue water, representing cold, dense ocean water, will stay at the bottom of the container.

Fig. 6: Use a straw to blow "wind" across the surface of the water.

THE SCIENCE BEHIND THE FUN

LAB
1

Alexander von Humboldt measured sea and air temperature on his voyages. In 1846, he wrote about a cold, low-salinity (salt) ocean current that flows north from Antarctica, along the west coast of South America. The current, named after Humboldt, is also called the Peru Current.

When wind blows across the surface of the ocean, it pushes on the water. This allows water to rise from under the surface to replace the water that was pushed away, carrying nutrients from the bottom. This phenomenon is called "upwelling." Upwelling occurs in the open ocean and along coastlines, providing food for plankton, which are eaten by animals such as fish, which are then eaten by larger fish, sea mammals, and birds. The Humboldt Current is one of the most productive ecosystems in the world.

Cold water is denser (heavier) than warm water. In this lab, you use ice water to represent the icy water that sits underneath warmer water in Antarctica. When you blow on the surface of the water, you can see how cold blue water rises from the bottom to mix with the warmer water above.

COLD CURRENTS 13

LAB 2

Eunice Newton Foote

(b. 1819)

A FAMOUS RELATIVE

Eunice Newton was born in 1819 in Goshen, Connecticut. She had six sisters and five brothers, and her father was a distant relative of the famous scientist Sir Isaac Newton. Eunice grew up in Bloomfield, New York, and attended Troy Female Seminary, which is now called the Willard School. She took chemistry and biology classes at a nearby science college, where she learned about physics and chemistry.

SUFFRAGETTE

Newton married Elisha Foote, who was an inventor, mathematician, and judge, and they had a daughter who would grow up to be an artist, writer, and social activist. In 1848, Eunice attended the first women's rights conference in America and signed a document called the "Declaration of Sentiments." The declaration, written by Eunice's friend Elizabeth Cady Stanton, called for equality with men and the right for women to vote.

AT-HOME SCIENTIST

During the nineteenth century, only sixteen physics papers were published by American women and two of those papers were written by Eunice Newton Foote. Although she didn't have a lab, Eunice did science at home. She was interested in many things, including how sunlight interacted with different gases. Using an air pump, two glass jars, and thermometers, she compared how the temperature inside the jars changed when they were filled with dry air, moist air, carbon dioxide (CO_2), or hydrogen and placed in the sunlight.

HEATING AND COOLING

Her research showed that carbon dioxide gas caused the temperature in the jar to rise the most. Eunice wrote, "The receiver containing this gas became itself much heated—very sensibly more so than the other—and on being removed [from sunlight] it was many times as long in cooling." She also found that the heating effect of moist air was greater than that of dry air and concluded, "An atmosphere of that gas [CO_2] would give to our Earth a high temperature."

GREENHOUSE GAS AND CLIMATE

Eunice's paper, "Circumstances Affecting the Heat of the Sun's Rays," was summarized in several journals. Unfortunately, most of them ignored her conclusion that gases we now call "greenhouse gases," such as carbon dioxide, can impact Earth's climate. Her research on sunlight, trapped gases, and water vapor was groundbreaking. Although she was the first person to propose a connection between carbon dioxide and climate change, she wasn't recognized for this accomplishment until 2010, when a geologist named Ray Sorenson came across her work in an old journal.

AN INVENTOR

Eunice Newton Foote continued to study gases and later published a paper on atmospheric pressure and electrical charges. In addition to research, she invented things with her husband. Their inventions included a new type of papermaking machine and a squeakless sole for shoes, made from a single piece of rubber.

GREENHOUSE GASES

Perform a greenhouse gas experiment by trapping the sun's energy in plastic bags.

MATERIALS

- 4 identical jars
- Water
- 20 ice cubes
- 3 large sealable clear plastic zip-top bags
- Black paper
- White paper
- Black-and-white newspaper or magazine pages
- Thermometer (glass or metal)

SAFETY TIPS AND HINTS

This experiment will work best on a sunny day.

PROTOCOL

1 Fill four jars halfway with water so that each jar contains the same volume. *Fig. 1*

2 Add five ice cubes to each jar. *Fig. 2*

3 Place three of the jars inside a plastic zip-top bag. Seal the bags.

4 Find a sunny spot outdoors. Set one bagged jar on black paper, one bagged jar on white paper, and the last two jars (one in a bag and one with no bag) on black-and-white newspaper or magazine pages. *Fig. 3*

5 After one hour, measure the water temperature in each of the jars and record the temperature. Reseal the jars in the bags. *Fig. 4*, *Fig. 5*

6 Wait an hour and measure the temperature again. *Fig. 6*

Fig. 6: Wait an hour and check the temperature again.

Fig. 1: Add an equal volume of water to four jars.

Fig. 2: Add five ice cubes to each jar.

Fig. 3: Seal three of the jars in plastic zip-top bags. Put the jars on light or dark paper.

Fig. 4: After one hour, measure the temperature in each jar.

Fig. 5: Record the temperature.

CREATIVE ENRICHMENT

Think of ways that you can reduce the amount of greenhouse gas you put into the atmosphere. Join an environmental club or create a personal plan for using less fossil fuel by turning out lights, unplugging unused appliances, carpooling, walking, and biking.

THE SCIENCE BEHIND THE FUN

Earth's atmosphere is a planetary blanket of gases, including nitrogen, oxygen, and heat-trapping greenhouse gases such as carbon dioxide and methane. Energetic ultraviolet rays from the sun constantly pass through the atmosphere. While some of the rays are reflected into space by white surfaces like polar ice caps, others are absorbed by dark surfaces and turned into heat energy. This heat can't easily escape back through the layer of greenhouse gases.

The clear plastic bags in this experiment represent greenhouse gases in Earth's atmosphere. Sunlight passes through the plastic, where it is turned into heat energy, which can't escape. You will probably observe that white surfaces reflect some of the sun's energy back into space, while dark paper absorbs the ultraviolet rays to produce more heat.

Oceans and trees absorb some of the carbon dioxide produced by burning fossil fuels, but human dependence on coal and oil has added too much greenhouse gas to Earth's atmosphere, resulting in global warming. This change to the climate is disrupting weather and damaging delicate ecosystems such as coral reefs and arctic tundra.

Jean-Henri Fabre

(b. 1823)

A BOOK LOVER

In 1823, Jean-Henri Fabre was born in Saint-Léons, a town in Aveyron, France. Although his family was extremely poor, Jean-Henri was born with the gift of curiosity and managed to educate himself by reading books and observing nature when a formal education wasn't possible. When he was nineteen, he was awarded a teaching certificate and worked as an educator as he continued to study. Eventually, he ended up teaching in Avignon, France, before moving to the region of Provence.

THE LIFE OF INSECTS

Jean-Henri was well known for being an extraordinary teacher. He studied physics, chemistry, and botany (the science of plants) but discovered that his true love lay in the study of insects. "A living speck—the merest dab of life— capable of pleasure and pain, is far more interesting to me than all the immensities of mere matter," he once wrote. Jean-Henri scrutinized the life of insects as few had before him, spending countless hours observing them in nature and in containers on tabletops.

FALLING SPARKS

In 1879, Jean-Henri began publishing a series of books called *Souvenirs entomologiques*, describing the lives and behavior of insects and arachnids, such as spiders. His engaging writing style was unusual. Jean-Henri's love of science was obvious from his keen observations, and he wrote in a lively biographical style. In one book, he wrote, "Few insects enjoy more fame that the glow-worm, the curious little animal who celebrates the joy of life by lighting a lantern at its tail-end. We all know it, at least by name, even if we have not seen it roaming through the grass, like a spark fallen from the full moon."

A SILKEN TRAIL

In *The Life of a Caterpillar*, he famously wrote about the behavior of pine processionary caterpillars, which lay down a trail of silk for other caterpillars to follow, one after another. As he observed some of the caterpillars one day, they climbed onto the rim of a flowerpot and laid down a silken path along the rim. Jean-Henri then watched them follow the trail in a circle for seven days until they finally broke away to eat some pine needles he'd placed close by. Other books in his famous *Souvenirs* series include *The Hunting-Wasps* and *The Life of the Weevil*.

POPULAR SCIENCE

Although most people loved Jean-Henri's books and he made the study of insects popular, many scientists preferred a more serious, dry writing style and made fun of his writing. Fortunately, he ignored them and continued to publish insightful, wonderful books containing wonderful observations such as, "The spider's web is a glorious mathematical problem." Jean-Henri Fabre didn't become famous until he was eighty-five years old. He lived in Provence and continued to study insects until his death at the age of ninety-one.

INSECT HABITATS

Build an insect habitat to study isopod behavior.

MATERIALS

- Two ½-gallon (1.9 L) cardboard milk cartons or a rectangular plastic box and a piece of cardboard
- Ruler
- Scissors and/or utility knife
- Duct tape or masking tape
- Dirt or potting soil
- Sand (optional)
- 10–20 land isopods, commonly called sowbugs or pillbugs (instructions on finding them below)
- Black or brown construction paper

SAFETY TIPS AND HINTS

Land isopods don't bite or sting, so it is safe to handle them with bare hands.

Adult supervision is recommended when cutting holes.

If you live in an area with poisonous snakes, use caution turning over rocks and logs.

PROTOCOL

1 If using milk cartons, measure and cut the tops off around 4 inches (10 cm) from the bottom of the cartons. Cut identical holes into the side of each carton about ½ inch (1 cm) up from the bottom. The holes should be around 2 inches (5 cm) long and 1¼ inches (3 cm) high. Tape the cartons together so the holes line up to form a single opening. *Fig. 1*. If using a plastic container, cut a piece of cardboard so that it will snugly divide the container in half. Create an opening, around 2 inches (5 cm) wide and 1¼ inches (3 cm) high, on one side of the cardboard so isopods can move from one side of the box to the other. Tape the cardboard into the plastic container snugly.

Fig. 3: Put an equal number of isopods on each side of the bug house.

2 Create moist and dry habitats. Add damp soil to one side of the habitat and sand to the other side. (Alternately, add dry dirt to both sides and moisten the dirt on one side but not the other.) The dirt should be deep enough to allow the isopods to crawl back and forth easily between the two sides.

3 Collect ten to twenty isopods (sowbugs or pillbugs) from a yard or a park. (See photos.) The small gray crustaceans can often be found under rocks, paving stones, and pieces of wood on the ground. They are usually ¼ to ½ inch (6 to 12 mm) long with seven pairs of legs, and they don't bite. Some isopods can roll up into tiny balls when they feel threatened. *Fig. 2*

4 Use your fingers or a spoon to place an equal number of isopods on each side of the habitat and observe them for half an hour or so. After 30 minutes, record how many bugs are on the moist side and dry side of the environment. *Fig. 3*, *Fig. 4*

5 Cover the sandy side of the habitat with paper to darken it and observe how the isopods react over a 15-minute period.

6 Remove the paper and darken the soil side of the bug house. After 30 minutes, count the isopods on each side of the bug house to see which environment they prefer. Record the results. *Fig. 5*

7 Gently remove the isopods to another container and add damp soil to both sides of the habitat. Repeat the experiment, making one side dark by covering it with paper.

8 Release the isopods where you found them.

CREATIVE ENRICHMENT

Create other habitats for isopods to see which they prefer. For example, you could make one side of the habitat cold by placing ice cubes underneath.

Fig. 1: Cut holes in two cartons and tape them together so the holes connect to form a passage.

Fig. 2: Land isopods are very small and don't bite. Pick them up with your hands or a scoop.

Fig. 4: Observe the isopods as they move between the damp and dry habitats.

Fig. 5: Count how many isopods are on each side of the container after half an hour.

THE SCIENCE BEHIND THE FUN

Every living thing on Earth has evolved to survive in a specific environment. Some fish live in saltwater but will die in freshwater. In tide pools, many animals can survive briefly in the air but require some exposure to the waves. Other animals have adapted to live in very cold climates and have antifreeze proteins in their blood.

The word *microenvironment* refers to a small area with specific conditions, such as the ecosystem beneath a rotting log lying on the floor of a pine forest.

Pillbugs and sowbugs belong to the order Isopoda and are related to crayfish and lobsters. They are crustaceans, with hard, armor-like exoskeletons, segmented bodies, and jointed legs. Although they are the only crustaceans that spend their entire lives on land, terrestrial isopods have gills and require moisture to breathe. In this lab, you will probably observe them moving to dark, damp areas, where there is more water for their gills.

Eugenius Warming

(b. 1841)

THE JUTLAND PENINSULA

Eugenius Warming was born in 1841 on the small island Mando, one of the Wadden Sea Islands off the southwest coast of the Jutland Peninsula in Denmark. When he was young, his father died. He and his mother moved to Vejle, an ancient Danish town on the mainland that lies on a long sea inlet called a fjord. Eugenius attended school in Ribe and then went to study natural history at the University of Copenhagen.

AN EDUCATION

Eugenius took a break from his studies at the university to work for the Danish paleontologist Peter Wilhelm Lund in the tropical grasslands of Brazil, where he observed the plants, animals, and geology of the area. Returning to Denmark, he obtained his PhD and became a professor at the University of Copenhagen and the director of their botanical gardens. He stayed in Demark for nine years and then moved to Sweden to become a botany professor at the Royal Institution in Stockholm.

ADVENTURES ABROAD

Fiercely curious about plants in other parts of the world, Eugenius traveled to Venezuela, the Caribbean, Greenland, Norway, and Denmark's rugged Faroe Islands. Believing that his students needed to observe plants in their natural habitats, he often took them on excursions. He was very popular with his students.

LIFE-FORMS

Eugenius wrote a number of popular books about his observations and ideas. He discovered hundreds of plant species that had not been described in European texts and wrote about how plants have adapted to live in different conditions, such as dunes, salt marshes, and other habitats. Eugenius was the first scientist to use the term *life-form*. He was interested in how environmental stress such as drought affected plants.

PLANTESAMFUND

Eugenius is often considered the founder of the scientific branch of ecology. His book *Plantesamfund* was the first introduction to all major biomes of the world and is the first textbook on plant ecology. A biome is a large, naturally occurring community of plants and animals that occupy a certain habitat, such as a forest, tundra, or desert. While botanists had always studied flora, or individual plant species, Eugenius studied vegetation, or entire plant communities. He demonstrated that living things respond to environmental stresses such as flooding, drought, salty water, and extreme temperatures in very similar ways in biomes all across the globe.

INFLUENCERS

Dr. Eugenius Warming was familiar with the work of two other important naturalists, Charles Darwin and Alfred Wallace, who studied how unique species developed as a result of adaptation to environmental stress. Darwin and Russell independently came up with the theory of evolution based on natural selection, which Darwin presented in his famous book, *On the Origin of Species*, in 1859.

EXPANDING CACTUS

Make a paper cactus to see how cacti expand when it rains.

MATERIALS
- Green craft paper
- Ruler
- Clear tape
- Tissue paper
- Waxed paper (optional)

SAFETY TIPS AND HINTS
Heavy paper works best for folding.

PROTOCOL

1 Lay paper in front of you vertically. Measure ½ inch (12 mm) up from the bottom and make a fold.

2 Flip the paper over so the fold is on top and fold it down to make an accordion fold. *Fig. 1*

3 Flip the paper again and again until the entire page is folded accordion style. *Fig. 2*

4 Open the paper and tape the two edges together to form a column representing a cactus. *Fig. 3*

5 Look up a photograph of a cactus flower and make one from tissue paper. *Fig. 4*

6 Squash the cylinder together to make it small. Imagine that this is a cactus living through a dry spell. *Fig. 5*

7 Now imagine that there is a thunderstorm and put your hand inside the cactus to illustrate how it can expand as the plant takes up water. *Fig. 6*

8 Draw spines on your cactus. *Fig. 7*

Fig. 5: Squash the cactus together to see how the stem contracts during a drought.

THE SCIENCE BEHIND THE FUN

Plants such as cacti have evolved to live in hot, dry desert ecosystems. They are very good at collecting water and holding on to it. Like other plants, they take water up through roots, but instead of leaves, they have spines that protect them from animals that want to eat them. The spines also help prevent drying out by reducing airflow around the cacti and produce some shade. Additionally, cacti have a waxy coating that keeps water inside to prevent them from drying out.

Most cacti use their stem as the main organ for storing water. They can be arborescent (branched like a tree), columnar (in column form), or globular (globe shaped). Although stem shapes vary, they are all optimal for storing water, which can form up to 90 percent of the mass of a cactus. In this lab, you can see how the ribbed or fluted stems of many cacti allow them to shrink in drought and swell when water is available. Mature saguaro cacti grow to be 10–52 feet (3–16 m) tall and can absorb up to 200 gallons (760 L) of water.

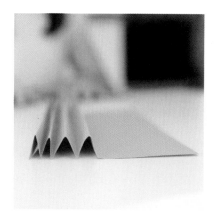

Fig. 1: Fold green paper using an accordion fold.

Fig. 2: The folds represent the ribbed stem of a cactus.

Fig. 3: Tape the paper together to form a column.

Fig. 4: Tissue paper can be used to make cactus flowers.

Fig. 6: Expand the folds to see how a cactus expands when it is full of water.

Fig. 7: Draw spines on your cactus.

CREATIVE ENRICHMENT

Drip water on some waxed paper to see how the waxy coating on cacti help them retain water.

William Emerson Ritter

(b. 1856)

A FARM BOY

William Emerson Ritter grew up on a farm in Wisconsin, where he first learned to love nature. Born in 1856, he and his family worked hard to survive, growing wheat, corn, apples, and potatoes, among other crops. William didn't go to high school until he was twenty. After a year, he started teaching and then attended college for a year but had to drop out because he couldn't afford it. He started teaching again and discovered a love for science, which he saw as a path to a better future.

GOBY FISH

Eventually, William went back to college, still teaching to earn money for tuition. He finally earned his college degree when he was thirty-two years old. He went to Harvard University, where he got a PhD in zoology (the study of animals) and got a teaching job at the University of California in Berkeley, where he became the chair of their new zoology department. While at Berkeley, he met Dr. Mary Bennett, a brilliant physician who became his wife. On their honeymoon in San Diego, they spent part of their time doing marine biology research by catching blind goby fish in the ocean.

SCRIPPS INSTITUTE

Fascinated by marine life, William and some students went on a two-month sea voyage to Alaska called the Harriman Expedition and studied marine creatures in their natural habitats along the coast of California, establishing temporary camps in several spots. However, he dreamed of teaching and doing research at a permanent marine station on the coast. This dream came true when his wealthy friend, E. W. Scripps, and his sister, Ellen Browning Scripps, bought land in La Jolla, California, in 1903. In 1907, they built the first building on the site where the Scripps Institute of Oceanography stands today.

ORGANICISM

When William was doing his research, most scientists only did research in the laboratory, but William believed that studying living things in their natural environments was the best way to understand the processes of life. He studied the eyes of lizards and fish and collected invertebrates such as marine worms. William believed that to understand life, we had to look at the big picture. He used the word *organicism* to describe life as a system composed of a complex web of interrelationships among chemicals, cells, organs, and organisms.

A PHILOSOPHER

Until his death at the age of eighty-one, William Emerson Ritter continued to study marine biology and focus on science education. Rather than observing the world from a single perspective, he was interested in the intersection of philosophy (the nature of knowledge and existence), zoology, evolution, and human nature as he tried to visualize larger systems at work. One of his colleagues wrote, "William E. Ritter looms large, not only as a most lovable personality but as a scientist of much originality and forcefulness."

INVERTEBRATES

Capture invertebrates in their natural habitats.

MATERIALS

- Garden trowel or shovel
- Collection container (cup, bucket, can, or plastic container)
- Plastic lid slightly larger than container (optional)
- White cloth or towel
- Magnifying glass
- 1–2 kitchen strainers with various mesh sizes
- White bowl or tray
- Plastic spoons, forces, or tweezers
- Empty ice cube tray
- Aquarium net (optional)

SAFETY TIPS AND HINTS

Adult supervision is recommended near water.

Don't dig where power lines might be buried.

Avoid picking up biting or stinging insects such as spiders with bare hands.

Small children should wear life jackets near lakes and ponds.

PITFALL TRAP PROTOCOL

1 Select a spot for your pitfall trap. You'll probably catch more insects in shady spots than in direct sunlight. Gardens and areas near trees are good places to sample arthropod populations. *Fig. 1*

2 Use a shovel or trowel to dig a hole for your collection container. The hole should be slightly deeper than the container. *Fig. 2*

Fig. 4: Place a lid over the pitfall trap and weight it down with rocks. Leave a large gap so that insects and arachnids can fall into the trap.

3 Place the collection container in the hole and fill in spaces on the side of the container with dirt so that the top of the container is flush with the surrounding soil. Use leaves or grass to camouflage the edges of the container.

4 To keep water out of the trap, set rocks or sticks around the edges of the container and balance a lid on top, leaving a large gap. Weight the lid down with rocks. *Fig. 3*, *Fig. 4*

5 Check the pitfall trap daily. Shake the invertebrates you catch onto a white cloth or towel. Photograph the arthropods and observe them under a magnifying glass. *Fig. 5*

6 Record your findings in a nature journal. Record the date, time, weather, location, what you caught, and how many of each species you captured. Include details about the size, number of legs, and appearance of each arthropod.

7 Using your photographs, descriptions, and an online resource or app, try to identify the arthropods.

8 Release the bugs where you caught them.

Fig. I: Find a shady, out-of-the-way spot for a pitfall trap.

Fig. 2: Dig a hole for a collection container.

Fig. 3: Put a few rocks or sticks around the hole to elevate the lid.

CREATIVE ENRICHMENT

To find terrestrial (land) invertebrates in the soil, dig up some dirt near a rock, log, or plant. Use a colander as a soil sieve, sifting the dirt through the screen over a white bowl or tray.

Fig. 5: Check the trap every day and then release the insects and arachnids you catch.

project continues ▶

LAB
5

WATER AND SOIL SIEVE PROTOCOL

1 Find a safe collection spot at the water's edge of a pond, stream, or beach. Use a kitchen sieve to scoop up sand and mud. *Fig. 1*, *Fig. 2*

2 Place the kitchen sieve over a white bowl or tray. If you have a larger sieve, dump the muck onto the larger mesh to look for small invertebrates dropping through the screen onto the surface below. *Fig. 3*. You can also dump your sample directly onto a white tray or bowl to watch for movement.

3 Use spoons or tweezers to gently collect invertebrates from your sample. Place larger invertebrates, like snails, clams, or crayfish, in a bowl or bucket with some lake, pond, or stream water. Smaller invertebrates may be sorted into ice cube trays.

4 If you have a net, use it to catch more aquatic invertebrates. Place them in a container of lake or pond water for observation. Use spoons or nets to handle larger invertebrates. *Fig. 4*, *Fig. 5*, *Fig. 6*

5 Observe the invertebrates with a magnifying glass and photograph them. In a notebook, record details about the invertebrates and how they move. Note any unusual features. Record the date, time, weather, location, and what you caught. *Fig. 7*

6 Use an online resource such as an app or a macroinvertebrate identification key (stroudcenter.org) to identify some of the invertebrates. *Fig. 8*

7 Release the invertebrates in the same spot where you captured them.

Fig. 1: Use a kitchen sieve to scoop sand and mud from a pond or lake bottom.

Fig. 2: Look for movement in the muck.

Fig. 3: Place the sieve on a white tray or bowl to catch small invertebrates that wriggle through the holes.

Fig. 4: Aquarium nets are useful for catching aquatic organisms.

Fig. 5: Fill a container with lake or pond water to hold what you catch.

Fig. 6: Use spoons or nets to handle larger invertebrates such as snails, clams, or crayfish.

Fig. 7: Observe the animals you catch under a magnifying glass.

Fig. 8: Try to identify the species you capture.

THE SCIENCE BEHIND THE FUN

Macroinvertebrates are animals without backbones that can be seen without using a microscope and include insects, arachnids, worms, and mollusks, such as clams and snails. Although many of them are very small, they play an essential role in ecosystems. Besides consuming algae, plants, and other animals, macroinvertebrates serve as nutrition for carnivores and omnivores higher up on the food chain. It is not surprising that changing macroinvertebrate populations can have a noticeable effect on bird and bat populations.

Some ecologists do regular invertebrate surveys in their research. The diversity and numbers of macroinvertebrates provide clues about water quality and the overall health of an ecosystem. In this lab, we use a few of the methods utilized by scientists working in the field. Pitfall traps, aquatic sieves, and soil sieves are all good ways to observe the local populations of these fascinating creatures.

George Washington Carver

(b. 1864)

BORN ENSLAVED

George Washington Carver was born enslaved in Diamond, Missouri, around 1864. His parents, Mary and Giles, had been purchased by a slave owner named Moses Carver in 1855, for seven hundred dollars. George's father died just before he was born, and when he was one week old, he was kidnapped by night raiders from Arkansas, along with his mother, sister, and brother. The raiders intended to sell George and his family as slaves in Kentucky. Moses Carver got George and his brother back, but their mother and sister were never found.

A NEW NAME

When slavery was abolished in 1865, Moses and his wife Susan raised George and his brother James as their own and taught them to read and write. Black people were not allowed at the school in Diamond, so George went to school in a town 10 miles (16 km) away, where he rented a room from a woman named Mariah Watkins. She suggested that he change his name from Carver's George (an enslaved name) to George Carver. She also suggested that he learn as much as possible and then share his learning with the world. Her words influenced him greatly.

A BRILLIANT STUDENT

George graduated from high school in Kansas but was denied college admission because of his race, so he home-steaded some land and planted crops. Eventually, he was able to get a loan to attend Simpson College in Iowa to study art and piano. His art teacher recognized his brilliance and suggested he apply to study botany at Iowa State University, where he became the first Black student in 1891. He earned a master's degree in science and became the university's first Black faculty member.

PRACTICE FARMS

In 1896, Booker T. Washington invited George to be the head of the agriculture department at Tuskegee University. George taught there for forty-seven years, but when he first arrived, he was not given a laboratory. Never one to give up easily, he took his students outdoors and to junkyards to find what they needed for their research, telling them to use what they had around them. They eventually set up practice farms on a 10-acre (4 ha) plot of land and built a station for doing experiments.

PUBLIC EDUCATION

George was passionate about educating the public, as well as his students. He reached out to the community and helped local farmers. Many grew cotton and were struggling with poor crops due to a pest called the boll weevil and soil depleted of nutrients from years of growing the same crop over and over. George taught them new techniques he'd created for rotating crops, by changing what they grew each season on the same piece of land.

SOIL TESTING

In addition to crop rotation, George suggested that farmers test their soil and water. He also advised people to grow new types of crops, such as sweet potatoes and peanuts, which were resistant to boll weevils and provided nutrition during hard times. George invented several new food products that could be prepared using peanuts. To teach farmers about his ideas, he wrote simple brochures that included information for growing crops and recipes for nutritious meals. George even created a mobile classroom for education, called the Jesup Wagon, which traveled through the countryside filled with plants.

AN EARLY ENVIRONMENTALIST

George Washington Carver was an artist, a botanist, an inventor, and an educator. He was interested in the ecology of farming, and his methods of crop rotation improved the health of the land, making him an early environmentalist. His hard life inspired him to want to help others. He once said, "It is not the style of clothes one wears, neither the kind of automobile one drives nor the amount of money one has in the bank that counts. These mean nothing. It is simply service that measures success."

SOIL CONDITIONS

Grow beans under different soil conditions.

MATERIALS

- 6 small flowerpots or gardening containers
- Vegetable potting soil or garden soil
- Clothespins or other labels
- Permanent marker
- Measuring spoons
- Baking soda
- Vinegar
- Peat moss
- Sand
- Zester or grater
- Lemon or orange
- Garden bush or pole bean seeds
- Support for pole beans if needed

SAFETY TIPS AND HINTS

Beans grow best in warm weather and warm soil.

Fig. 7: When the beans are tall, add supports or transplant them.

PROTOCOL

1 Fill the pots or containers with soil. Use the same source of soil for all containers.

2 Use the clothespins and marker to label the pots "control," "baking soda," "vinegar," "peat moss," "sand," and "citrus peel." *Fig. I*

3 Add ½ teaspoon of baking soda to the soil of the "baking soda" pot and mix well. *Fig. 2*

4 Pour I tablespoon (15 ml) of vinegar over the "vinegar" pot and mix into the soil.

5 Remove a handful of soil from the "peat moss" pot and replace it with the same amount of peat moss. Mix well.

6 Remove a handful of soil from the "sand" pot and replace it with sand. Mix well.

7 Grate the peel of a lemon or orange and mix it into the soil of the "citrus peel" pot. *Fig. 3*

8 Plant three beans in each pot, following the directions on the label for planting depth and seed distance. *Fig. 4*

9 Water the soil until it is damp. *Fig. 5*

10 Place the pots in a sunny place and water as needed to keep the soil damp, but not wet.

11 Record the progress of the beans as they grow, noting date, height, color, and health of the seedlings. *Fig. 6*

12 Add support to pole bean seedlings or transplant them into a planting box or garden. *Fig. 7*

13 When the beans are ready to pick, record how many beans you harvest from each pot.

CREATIVE ENRICHMENT

Use what you learned from the experiment to create the best possible soil conditions for growing beans.

Fig. 1: Add soil to six planting containers and label "control," "baking soda," "vinegar," "peat moss," "sand," and "citrus peel."

Fig. 2: Add approximately ½ teaspoon of baking soda to the soil in the baking soda pot and mix well.

Fig. 3: Grate lemon or orange peel into the "citrus peel" pot and mix.

Fig. 4: Plant three beans in each container.

Fig. 5: Water the beans.

Fig. 6: Record the progress of the beans as they grow.

THE SCIENCE BEHIND THE FUN

Legumes are plants with pods and seeds that are members of the pea family, *Fabaceae*. Green beans, black beans, kidney beans, and peanuts are all legumes. These plants play an essential role in ecosystems because they live in a symbiotic relationship with the soil bacteria, rhizobacteria (rise-oh-bacteria), which means that they both get something out of the relationship. These bacteria live on the roots of plants and capture nitrogen gas from the atmosphere, which is called "fixing" nitrogen. Rhizobacteria feed this nitrogen to legumes in exchange for the plants' carbohydrates, enriching the soil with nitrogen.

George Washington Carver understood that certain crops, such as peanuts, improve the soil for other crops that are planted later in the same fields. In addition to crop rotation, George suggested that farmers test their soil and water and adjust nutrients and soil acidity. In this lab, you test how well the beans grow under different soil conditions. Adding vinegar, lemon peel, or peat moss makes soil more acidic, while adding baking soda makes it less acidic. It is easier for water to move through sandy soil, but nutrients can be washed away more easily.

Ed Ricketts

(b. 1897)

A BUDDING ZOOLOGIST

Ed Ricketts was born in Chicago in 1897. When he was six years old, his uncle gave him some natural history curios and an old zoology textbook. From that moment on, he was hooked on animals. Later, in high school, he enjoyed studying the sciences and subjects like literature and history. However, college wasn't a good fit for him, and he dropped out to travel through the American Southwest before being drafted into the army for World War I.

ANIMAL AGGREGATIONS

When the war ended, Ed enrolled in the University of Chicago, where he was hugely influenced by a professor named Warder Clyde Allee, who was interested in the relationships between living things. Allee argued that all animals, including humans, instinctually aggregate (gather) into communities, where they cooperate to survive. Ed never graduated from college, but Allee's work provided a foundation that he built on when he moved to Monterey in California to start a company called Pacific Biological Labs with one of his college roommates.

PACIFIC BIOLOGICAL LABORATORIES

From his lab, Ed sold live and preserved animals to schools and universities. He often collected marine specimens from tide pools near his lab, discovering that you should never turn your back on the ocean, when a big wave almost carried him out to sea. Ed understood that it was important not to collect too many of any single species. When he turned a rock over, he always returned it to the original position so any animals attached to the rock wouldn't die.

INTERTIDAL ZONES

Ed was especially interested in invertebrates—animals with no backbones, such as hermit crabs, barnacles, starfish, sea urchins, and sea cucumbers. As he studied the tide pools, he watched the interactions among animals and noticed that he usually found certain species in specific tidal zones. Plants and animals that could survive drying out lived higher up on the shore, while those that lived in areas pummeled by waves were more tightly attached, and certain animals were only found submerged in the deepest zones, where they rarely encountered air.

BETWEEN PACIFIC TIDES

At that time, most books about invertebrates were mostly just lists of animals and their scientific names. Ed changed the way people observe and understand life in the tidal zones when he wrote a famous book called *Between Pacific Tides*. In language that both scientists and non-scientists can understand, he writes about life in tide pools in a way that is entertaining as well as educational. Ed arranges the animals according to where they live, from sandy beaches to rocky shores, and describes how they interact with the environment and each other. He described the big picture, which we now call ecology, before ecology was an official science.

CANNERY ROW

Ed loved art, classical music, jazz, psychology, history, and literature. Groups of friends would gather in his lab at night to play games, listen to music, and talk about the meaning of life. His author friend John Steinbeck often incorporated Ed into his stories. The character "Doc" in Steinbeck's book *Cannery Row* is based on Ed, although the author made some things up to make the story more entertaining. In 1940, John Steinbeck, Ed Ricketts, and Steinbeck's wife Carol went on a biological collecting trip in the Gulf of California, which is also called the Sea of Cortez. They collected hundreds of invertebrates, including some species that had never before been identified. When they returned, Steinbeck and Ed coauthored a book about the trip called *The Log from the Sea of Cortez*.

IN TODAY'S WORLD

Ed Ricketts inspired countless people to become marine biologists. His legacy continues today as the Western Flyer Foundation rebuilds the boat he and the Steinbecks took to the Sea of Cortez. The Western Flyer will be used as a research and education vessel.

TIDE POOL IN A TUB

Build a tide pool in a tub and make waves to see how changing water levels affect shoreline invertebrates.

MATERIALS

- Playdough or sculpting clay
- Several medium to small rocks
- A medium or large clear plastic bin
- Scissors
- Toothpicks
- Containers for pouring and scooping water
- Rectangular plastic lid
- Tape
- Plastic tubing (optional)
- Empty plastic bottle with a hole in the lid (optional; a hole can easily be made using a nail and hammer)

SAFETY TIPS AND HINTS

Younger kids may need help attaching animals to the rocks.

Playdough will dissolve slightly in water, so if you want perfectly clear water in your tide pool, use sculpting clay.

Always supervise young children around containers full of water.

PROTOCOL

1 Look up an image of a rocky intertidal zone and study it to see which animals live in the different zones.

2 Use playdough or sculpting clay to attach several rocks to the bottom of one end of a clear plastic container. Create a rock wall that slants down from the container's end, representing a rocky intertidal zone. From top to bottom are the splash zone, the high intertidal zone, the middle intertidal zone, and the low intertidal zone.

Fig. 3: Limpets, periwinkles, hermit crabs, sea anemones, sea stars, barnacles, urchins, mussels, and algae live in rocky tidal pools.

3 Use playdough or sculpting clay to create limpets, periwinkles, chitins, hermit crabs, sea anemones, sea stars, big and small barnacles, sea urchins, and mussels. Scissors and toothpicks will help create details. *Fig. 1*

4 Use toothpicks to secure the lifeforms you made in the intertidal zones, where they are likely to be found. Limpets and periwinkles are normally found at the very top in the splash zone; limpets, periwinkles, and small barnacles a little farther down in the high intertidal; hermit crabs, mussels, anemones, and large barnacles further down in the middle intertidal; and large sea anemones, sea urchins, and sea stars on the low intertidal, near the bottom. *Fig. 2*, *Fig. 3*

5 Add water to the container by pouring it on the end opposite the rocks so that it just covers the animals in the low intertidal zone. Note which animals are wet and which are exposed to the air during low tides. *Fig. 4*

6 Slowly add more water to the container to represent the tide coming in until it covers the animals in the middle intertidal zone. Note which animals are wet and which are still exposed to the air as the tide comes in.

7 Use a rectangular plastic lid to make waves splash against the rocky shore. What happens to the animals in each zone? *Fig. 5*

8 Add more water so that it covers all but the animals on the highest rocks to represent high tide. Notice which animals get wet when you make waves.

9 Scoop the water out or use a siphon (see step II) to make the tide go out again. Think about how long each animal is exposed to the water.

10 Consider the following questions: Which zones require animals to be most tightly attached? Which animals must be resistant to drying out? How would animals living in exposed intertidal zones with wind and large waves differ from those living in a protected area, such as a bay?

11 Optional: To use a siphon, use tape to secure one end of a long piece of tubing at the bottom of the tub of water. The end outside the container must be lower than the water. Put a large collection bottle under the siphon. Place the lower end of the tubing securely over the hole in the lid of the plastic bottle and squeeze several times to create suction. The water should start to flow out of the container through the tube.

Fig. I: Make tide pool animals and plants to inhabit different intertidal zones.

Fig. 2: Use toothpicks to attach tide pool creatures to the rocks.

Fig. 4: Add water to the tide pool, a little at a time, to represent low tide, the incoming tide, and high tide.

Fig. 5: Make waves in the container to see how wave shock affects animals.

CREATIVE ENRICHMENT

If you live near the ocean or will visit an area with tide pools, sign up for a citizen science project, such as Tide Pool Citizen Science (https://scistarter. org/tide-pool-citizen-science), which allows you to document the plants and animals you observe for research. Only visit tide pools with an adult and make safety your top priority. Do not touch the animals and if you turn a rock over, always flip it back over. Be very careful not to step on animals and remember Ed Ricketts's advice: "Never turn your back on the ocean."

THE SCIENCE BEHIND THE FUN

Tides are a result of the moon's gravitational pull on Earth's water, and many living creatures have evolved to live in areas regularly covered and uncovered by tides. Ed Ricketts wrote that three things determine where invertebrates live on the shores of the ocean: "wave shock," which refers to the physical force of ocean waves as they hit the shore; what the bottom is made of; and tidal exposure, which refers to how long living organisms are exposed to water and air.

He divided the types of shore habits into four areas: protected outer coast, where animals are slightly protected from the ocean; open coast, which is pounded by ocean waves; bays and estuaries, where the tide rises and falls but animals are not exposed to the surf; and wharf pilings on docks, where numerous animal communities live.

Ed called the splash zone "zone I," the uppermost beach. It rarely gets wet, except during storms and the highest tides. Zone 2 is the high intertidal, where animals such as barnacles that can tolerate more air than water live. In the middle intertidal, zone 3, animals require being covered and uncovered by tides to survive. Zone 4, the low intertidal, is uncovered only during the lowest tides, and animals there cannot tolerate too much air exposure.

G. Evelyn Hutchinson

(b. 1903)

A TRICKSTER

G. Evelyn Hutchinson was born in 1903 and grew up in Cambridge, in the United Kingdom, near the university where his father taught minerology. With one brother and one sister, he was surrounded by other children whose parents worked at the university. Evelyn was mischievous and liked to play pranks on his friends, including the sons of famous scientist Charles Darwin. By the time he was five, Evelyn was catching aquatic creatures from ponds and keeping them in homemade aquariums.

A NEW ENVIRONMENT

The school Evelyn attended focused on science, math, modern languages, and history. In his early years of studying plants, animals, and chemistry, he was fascinated by the fact that different organisms live in different chemical environments. Zoology (the study of animals) became Evelyn's focus in college.

A LUCKY BREAK

After college, Evelyn went to Italy to study octopuses, but there was an octopus shortage and he had to change plans. He traveled to South Africa, where he studied the chemistry and biology of coastal lakes with the biologist Grace E. Pickford, who later became his wife for three years. They both ended up at Yale University in New Haven, Connecticut, where she got her doctorate degree. He applied for graduate student fellowships, but luck intervened and he was appointed as a faculty lecturer in zoology, giving him the freedom to continue with his own research.

LINLEY POND

Based on his observations, Evelyn came up with a famous theory called the "niche theory," which states that an organism's ecological niche is a description of its role in the natural environment: how it survives, how it acquires food and shelter, and how it interacts with other organisms. He continued studying freshwater systems, focusing on Linley Pond in North Branford, Connecticut. Evelyn was curious about how the chemistry and temperature of the pond affected the populations of animals, such as plankton and water bugs, that lived in there. He wondered how the animal populations could be so different in ponds that looked alike.

PARADOX OF THE PLANKTON

To understand the forces at work, he and his students started taking measurements. They measured the chemical composition of the pond water through the seasons over several years and kept track of the animal populations to see how the two things were related. At that time, most people thought that when food was scarce in a contained area like a pond, one species would take over, but Evelyn discovered that this wasn't true with plankton and wrote a paper about it.

COMMUNITY

Through his research, G. Evelyn Hutchinson observed and measured the effects that climate and chemistry have on plant and animal populations in communities collectively called ecosystems. Because he was one of the first to take these measurements, he is considered a pioneer of modern ecology. Evelyn was a beloved teacher and mentor to his students and understood the importance of his role as a teacher. On the door of his office, he hung a sign that said, "Never discourage a student, for you are sure to succeed."

PLANKTON POPULATION

Use a plastic bottle and nylons to capture plankton.

MATERIALS

- Marker
- Empty plastic soda or water bottle with a cap
- Scissors
- Pair of nylons (pantyhose)
- Duct tape or clear packing tape
- Hole punch (optional)
- String or twine
- Access to a floating dock or dock close to the water
- Magnifying glass or microscope
- Collection container, such as a jar
- Notebook

SAFETY TIPS AND HINTS

Floating docks and docks low to the water are the best places to collect plankton safely.

Adult supervision is always required when collecting samples. For safety, avoid fast-moving rivers or streams.

PROTOCOL

1 With a marker, draw a line about I inch (2.5 cm) above the bottom of the bottle and a second line around two-thirds of the way up. Use scissors to punch a hole in the bottle and cut along the lines.

2 Recycle the bottom of the bottle and save the other two pieces, including the bottle cap.

3 Cut the toe off the nylons and then make another cut so that you have a 6-inch (15 cm) long piece of nylon.

Fig. 4: Squeeze the nylon to move any plankton to the mouth of the bottle.

4 Use the nylon tube to connect the two pieces of bottle by stretching the nylon over the edges of the bottle pieces. The open end is the mouth of the plankton net, the nylon is the "belly," and the section with the lid is the "cod" end, where the sample is collected.

5 Use tape to secure the nylon to the bottle. *Fig. I*

6 Use a hole punch or scissors to make three holes, approximately equal distance apart, on the rim of the mouth of the bottle.

7 Cut three pieces of string or twine so that they are around I yard (91 cm) long. Securely tie the end of each string to one of the holes in the plankton net. Tie the three strings together at the opposite end. *Fig. 2*

8 Find a safe collection spot, such as a floating dock or dock low to the water. Collect plankton by dragging the net through the water several times, being careful not to scoop sand or muck from the bottom. *Fig. 3*

9 Gently squeeze the nylon toward the cod end of the bottle to move any plankton caught on the nylon. Study the water in the cod (mouth) end to look for movement. Use a magnifying glass, if you have one. *Fig. 4*

10 Hold the cod (mouth) end of the net, lid side down, over the collection container and open the bottle lid to release the plankton into the container. *Fig. 5*

11 Use a magnifying glass or microscope to observe the plankton. Search for a website or app to aid in plankton identification. Record the date, time of day, weather, location, and what you found.

CREATIVE ENRICHMENT

Capture plankton at the same spot over several weeks or months to study how the population changes.

Fig. 1: Use waterproof tape and a section of nylon stocking to connect the two pieces of bottle.

Fig. 2: Punch holes and tie three long strings to the open end of the plankton net.

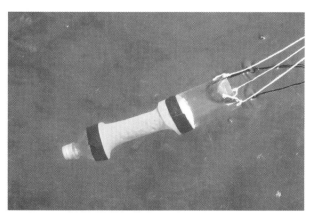

Fig. 3: Collect plankton by dragging the net through the water, keeping the open end under water.

Fig. 5: Hold the mouth of the bottle over a container and remove the lid to collect your sample.

THE SCIENCE BEHIND THE FUN

Plankton are drifters and floaters, rather than swimmers. In fact, the word *plankton* is derived from the Greek adjective *planktos*, which means "wanderer." While some plankton are microscopic, full-grown jellyfish are also considered plankton. These living organisms depend on tides, currents, and winds to get from one place to another. They are an essential part of aquatic ecosystems and provide food for larger animals, from barnacles to whales.

Some plankton spend their entire lives floating through the water. Others are larvae of animals such as sea urchins, starfish, worms, and fish, which eventually attach themselves to solid surfaces or swim against the current. Because phytoplankton are plants and zooplankton are animals, zooplankton often eat phytoplankton before being eaten by fish and other species higher in the food chain. In addition to providing food for zooplankton, phytoplankton use sunlight and carbon dioxide for energy, removing carbon dioxide from the atmosphere and producing much of Earth's oxygen.

Plankton are found in both freshwater and saltwater. Green, brown, or cloudy water usually contains more plankton than very clear water. Certain areas, such as the Gulf of Mexico, where whale sharks gather to feed on plankton, have beautifully murky blue-green water.

⹀ LAB 9 ⹀

Dora Priaulx Henry

(b. 1904)

A BIG MOVE

Dora Priaulx was born in Maquoketa, Iowa, in 1904. Both of her parents were teachers. After the death of her father, when she was five, her mother moved Dora and her brothers to Los Angeles. School came easily to Dora and she graduated from Hollywood High School before getting a biology degree from the University of California at Berkeley. Interested in parasites, she got a master's degree at Berkeley as well and married a fellow student named Bernard Henry.

FROM PARASITES TO BARNACLES

After completing her PhD in parasitology at UC Berkeley, Dora and Bernard moved to Seattle, where she began to study parasites called gregarines, which were infecting barnacles in Puget Sound. As she worked, her interest shifted from the parasites to the barnacles themselves. She started collecting barnacles, identifying them and writing papers about the fascinating invertebrates, which attach headfirst to boats, rocks, whales, crustaceans, and almost anything else in the water.

WORLD WAR II

The Smithsonian Institution in Washington, D.C., was impressed by Dora's expansive knowledge and encouraged her to study their museum barnacle collections. She was also an important consultant for Ed Ricketts (Lab 7) in his early work on intertidal ecology. Dora is mentioned in Ed's book *The Log from the Sea of Cortez*, which he wrote with the famous author John Steinbeck. Barnacle growth can present a big problem for ships, and World War II led Dora to work as an assistant oceanographer with the air force and then to the navy's Hydrographic Office.

TRAVEL ABROAD

Interested in the distribution patterns of barnacles, Dora was the first to accurately plot the range of places where they grew on a map. She continued to study barnacles until she was ninety-three years old. Her fieldwork took her from Lower California and the Gulf of California to the Gulf of Mexico, the Central Pacific Islands, and Bermuda. She discovered new species, learned new things about barnacle reproduction, and wrote countless papers.

AN EDUCATOR

Dr. Dora Priaulx Henry loved to travel. In 1968, she helped develop a "Coasts of the World" travel course, which took students and faculty to the South Pacific and South America to learn about wind, waves, tides, volcanoes, glaciers, beaches, and life in the intertidal and near-shore environments. She always welcomed visits from colleagues from around the word. Today, her barnacle collection can be found at the Smithsonian Institution's Museum of Natural History.

IN TODAY'S WORLD

Barnacles still present a challenge to boats, but researchers are very interested in the strong glue they make to cement themselves to wet objects very quickly. One group of researchers has copied their oily adhesive to make a substance that can be applied to wounds to quickly stop bleeding.

BARNACLE MODEL

Fabricate a moving model of a barnacle.

MATERIALS

- Small paper cup, such as a 3-ounce (85 ml) bathroom cup
- Marker
- Craft knife
- Paint (optional)
- Flowerpot with a large drainage hole in the bottom
- Glue gun or craft glue
- Ruler
- Scissors
- Yarn or string
- Duct tape
- Long dowel or skewer with the sharp end cut off
- Plastic bottle caps

Fig. 4: Use a piece of yarn to knot the other pieces of yarn together in the center.

SAFETY TIPS AND HINTS

Adult supervision is recommended for cuts made with a craft knife.

PROTOCOL

1 Turn a small paper cup over. Draw a line down the middle and along the edges of the cup, leaving two gaps parallel to the middle line. *Fig. 1*

2 Use a craft knife to make a cut through the center of the circular bottom. Create two hinged halves by cutting along the sides of the circle, leaving two uncut sections parallel to the cut in the center.

3 Paint the cut to look like an acorn barnacle (optional).

4 Turn the flowerpot upside down and use a glue gun or craft glue to firmly glue the cup to the flowerpot, rim-side down. This glue represents the strong cement made by barnacles. *Fig. 2*

5 With a ruler and scissors, measure and cut six pieces of yarn or string, each around 6 inches (15 cm) long. *Fig. 3*

6 Use a piece of yarn to knot the other pieces of yarn together in the center so that the knot is small enough to fit through the hole in the flowerpot. *Fig. 4*

7 Securely tape the knot to the dowel or skewer so that the pieces of yarn are pointing away from the dowel or skewer. *Fig. 5*

8 Push the yarn up through the hole in the flowerpot so that it is inside the cup.

9 To make the barnacle "cirre" (appendages) emerge, use the skewer to push the yarn through the two hinged flaps in the cup. Imagine the barnacle is using the cirre to capture food such as plankton. *Fig. 6*, *Fig. 7*

10 When threatened, barnacles pull their cirre back inside and close the protective top plates that function as armor. Pull the barnacle you made back inside of its protective shell.

CREATIVE ENRICHMENT

Look up photographs of different barnacles online. Draw the life cycle of an acorn barnacle.

Fig. 1: Draw a line down the middle and along the edges of a paper cup, leaving two gaps parallel to the middle line.

Fig. 2: Use a glue gun or craft glue to firmly glue the cup to the flowerpot, rim-side down.

Fig. 3: Cut six pieces of yarn or string, each around 6 inches (15 cm) long.

Fig. 5: Securely tape the knot to the dowel or skewer.

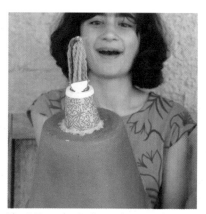

Fig. 6: To make the barnacle appendages emerge from the shell, push the yarn up through the hinged flaps in the cup.

Fig. 7: Wave the barnacle's cirre around as though it is catching microscopic food from the water.

THE SCIENCE BEHIND THE FUN

Barnacles are astonishing marine organisms that live with their heads cemented to objects such as rocks and whales, where they catch food with their legs. Most barnacles live inside of hard calcium shells, but they are crustaceans and are more closely related to lobsters than to clams. Acorn barnacles are some of the most common.

Before they settle down, barnacles are swimmers. The eggs and embryos of barnacles are discharged from within mature barnacles as free-swimming larvae called nauplii (nah-plee-eye). Each nauplius has one eye, one shell, and three legs. Each nauplius transforms into a cypris (sih-pris) with three eyes, two shells, and six pairs of legs before deciding to settle down permanently.

Once they find the perfect spot for a house, acorn barnacles use their antennae to grab on and produce a strong cement, gluing themselves down headfirst. They undergo another shape-shifting metamorphosis and emerge with eight pairs of long, feathery limbs called cirre, which filter food from the water. As they grow, barnacles build a cone-shaped shell made of six hard calcium plates that can open and close like a door, depending on the tide or the presence of predators.

Rachel Carson

(b. 1907)

A NATURE LOVER

Rachel Carson always wanted to be a writer and published her first article for a children's magazine when she was eleven. Born in Springdale, Pennsylvania, in 1907, she loved reading and exploring nature. The fields and woods near her house were filled with birds and other animals, although on some days, everything was coated with gray ash from steel mills that stood downriver from where she lived. Her family struggled to pay the bills, and Rachel's mother, Marie, gave piano lessons to help support Rachel and her two siblings.

AWAKENED BY BIRDS

Every morning, Rachel woke to hear the birds singing. She worked very hard in school, and in her senior paper for high school she wrote that a "thinking, reasoning mind" was a person's most valuable possession. Her parents sold off part of their land to help pay for her college. Rachel got a master's degree from Johns Hopkins University and spent time at the Marine Biological Laboratory in Woods Hole, Massachusetts, where she explored tide pools and fell in love with the sea.

AN AUTHOR

After graduating, Rachel found a job as a writer for the U.S. Department of Fish and Wildlife. Finding inspiration in the natural world, she started to write books about the sea, weaving in geology, chemistry, and biology. With words, she painted beautiful images of the intertidal zones and the open ocean, making science engaging and easy to understand. Inspired by Ed Ricketts's work (Lab 7), she organized her descriptions of marine ecosystems by zones, and by 1962, she was a best-selling author. Her poetic books on the ocean's ecosystems made her one of the most popular science writers of her time.

DDT

Near where Rachel worked in Maryland, a new pesticide (insect killer) called DDT was being tested for safety. Her job at the Department of Fish and Wildlife made her a witness to some of the first reports that DDT was also deadly to fish and wildlife populations. As she studied the data, it became clear to her that the chemical was killing more than mosquitos. Her background in science helped her understand that DDT could move through soil and water from the fields and wetlands where it had been sprayed into nearby lakes, streams, and rivers. The chemical moved up the food chain, from invertebrates into the bodies of fish, birds, and mammals, often killing them or making it harder for them to reproduce.

AN ACTIVIST FOR NATURE

When the government started spraying the DDT regularly around the United States, Rachel and many other people noticed the gradual disappearance of birds. She missed their song in springtime. In 1962, Rachel sparked the environmental movement with her famous book, *Silent Spring*, using scientific evidence to support her claim that DDT was harming ecosystems. She stood up to the huge corporations that were producing the chemical and telling the public that it was safe. She was bullied, ridiculed, and called "a spinster," "hysterical," and "an uninformed woman speaking of that which she did not know." But she persisted and DDT was banned. Rachel refused to be silent. Her words and her bravery eventually resulted in the ban of DDT in the United States.

IN TODAY'S WORLD

Rachel Carson reminded us that what we do to the environment, we do to ourselves. Many of today's ecologists study the impacts of human behavior on Earth's ecosystems, searching for ways we can maintain healthy relationships with other living things.

WATER CLARITY

Make a Secchi disk to test water clarity in a pond, lake, or reservoir.

MATERIALS

- Black duct tape
- White duct tape
- Old compact disc (CD)
- Scissors
- Nylon stockings (pantyhose)
- Rocks or marbles to use as weights
- Thin nylon rope several yards (m) long
- Yardstick
- Permanent marker or red duct tape

SAFETY TIPS AND HINTS

Floating docks and docks low to the water are good places to test water clarity. Results will be the best between 10 a.m. and 2 p.m. in the shade of a dock or boat.

Adult supervision is always required when collecting samples. Avoid fast-moving rivers or streams. Small children should wear life vests near the water.

PROTOCOL

1 To make a Secchi disk, add pieces of black and white duct tape to a compact disc or another circular object of around the same size so that it has four equal quadrants with white quadrants next to black quadrants. *Fig. 1*, *Fig. 2*

2 With scissors, cut off a nylon stocking so that the toe is intact. It should be at least 6 inches (15 cm) long. If the nylon doesn't have a toe, knot one end.

Fig. 12: Record the depth where the disk disappears and reappears.

3 Fill the toe of the nylon with several rocks or marbles to weight it down. *Fig. 3*

4 Make a hole in the center of the Secchi disk. Poke the stocking through the hole and knot the fabric. *Fig. 4*, *Fig. 5*, *Fig. 6*

5 Tie one end of the nylon rope firmly to the stocking, below the knot in the stocking. Tie it a few more times so that the Secchi disk cannot move up over the knot. *Fig. 7*

6 Starting at the Secchi disk, use a yardstick and marker to make marks on the nylon rope every 3 feet (1 m) until you get to the end of the line. (If you don't have a marker, use brightly colored duct tape or yarn, or tie knots every 3 feet [1 m].) *Fig. 8*

7 Try to find a spot in the shade of a dock or boat so you can see the Secchi disk as it descends. Note the wave size and cloud cover, which can affect your results. *Fig. 9*

Fig. I: Use black duct tape to cover opposite sides of a compact disc.

Fig. 2: Use white duct tape to add two triangular shapes so that the disc has four equal, opposite quadrants.

Fig. 3: Fill the toe of a nylon stocking with several rocks or marbles.

Fig. 4: Make a hole in the center of the disc.

8 Lower the Secchi disk slowly, until you can no longer see it. Keep an eye on the marks on the rope to record the depth. *Fig. 10*

9 Using the marks on the rope, record the approximate depth (Depth I) at the water line. *Fig. II*

10 Slowly raise the Secchi disk until it comes back into view and record that depth (Depth 2). *Fig. 12*

11 The Secchi reading is the average of the two depths. Calculate it by adding Depth I to Depth 2 and then dividing that number by two.

CREATIVE ENRICHMENT

Test the water quality of a pond or lake on a regular basis to see how it changes after storms and during algae blooms.

project continues ▶

Fig. 5: Pull the stocking through the hole.

Fig. 6: Knot the stocking.

Fig. 7: Tie one end of a nylon rope firmly to the stocking, below the knot in the stocking.

Fig. 8: Make marks on the nylon rope every 3 feet (1 m) until you get to the end of the line.

Fig. 9: Look for a spot in the shade of a dock or boat to test water clarity.

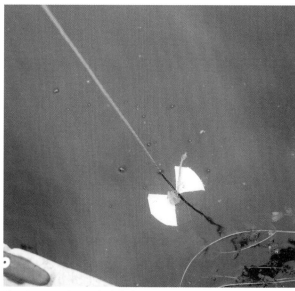

Fig. 10: Lower the Secchi disk slowly, until you can no longer see it.

Fig. 11: Use the marks to keep track of the depth.

THE SCIENCE BEHIND THE FUN

The Secchi disk was invented in 1865 by Angelo Secchi to measure the transparency or turbidity (cloudiness) of water in the Mediterranean Sea. Although the first Secchi disks were white, black-and-white Secchi disks are now standard tools for limnology, which is the study of inland aquatic ecosystems. Ecologists, wildlife biologists, and citizen scientists use Secchi disks to monitor the health of bodies of water around the world.

Water clarity reveals important things about the quality of aquatic ecosystems, including how much sunlight can travel through the water. Sunlight impacts water temperature and how much dissolved oxygen is available for fish and other aquatic organisms. Aquatic plants and phytoplankton need sunlight for photosynthesis, a chemical process that breaks down carbon dioxide and produces oxygen.

In the ocean, cloudy water is usually good. It often indicates the presence of plankton, which supports fish and marine mammal populations. However, in smaller freshwater systems, murky water can indicate the overgrowth of algae from farm runoff, fertilizer, and other pollutants. In the United States, volunteers in Minnesota, Wisconsin, and Indiana make periodic Secchi disk measurements in local lakes to track changes in water clarity.

Eugene Odum

(b. 1913)

THE BIG PICTURE

Eugene Odum, who was born in Newport, New Hampshire, in 1913, pioneered the term *ecosystems* as we understand it today. Eugene and his brother Howard were both interested in the plants and animals in the world around them. Their father, who was a professor of sociology, taught them that it was always important to look at the big picture before zooming in on details. This holistic approach to exploring the world and approaching problems played an important role in Eugene's education.

CHICKADEES

In 1939, Eugene got a doctorate degree (PhD) in zoology from the University of Illinois and married an artist named Martha Ann Huff. They move to Rensselaerville, New York, and Eugene went to work as a naturalist at a biological research station in the 430-acre (175 ha) Huyck nature preserve. While he was there, he prepared a habitat map of plants in the area and measured the chickadee population in shrubland versus different types of forest in the preserve.

FUNDAMENTALS OF ECOLOGY

The importance of studying entire ecosystems was on Eugene's mind when he went to work as a biology instructor at the University of Georgia. He suggested to the rest of the faculty there that the study of ecosystems, which he called ecology, should be required for all biology students. When the other professors laughed at the idea, it made him angry. He decided to write the first textbook ever about how living organisms and their environment impacted each other. This book, called *Fundamentals of Ecology*, became the foundation for modern ecology and thanks to Dr. Odum, the first department of ecology was founded at the University of Georgia.

THE FROG

Eugene liked to remind people that an ecosystem is more than the sum of its parts, and that it is essential that we always study the big picture. He famously said, "We would not first bring the student the liver of the frog, have him study that, then the next day bring him the isolated stomach or each individual muscle one by one—and finally during the last week of the course attempt to assemble all the parts into a frog," he wrote. "Our poor frog would be most incomplete and probably bear little resemblance to the real frog when we tried to assemble the parts we did study!"

OUR "BIG HOUSE"

Dr. Eugene Odum liked to remind students that the word *ecology* comes from the Greek word for "house." Because Eugene saw Earth as a global set of interlaced ecosystems, he continued to study the effect of human activities on global ecosystems. He worked to educate the public about the importance of protecting the environment, saying, "We must begin to devote more of our human wealth, energy, and engineering skills to servicing and repairing our 'big house,' the biosphere, which provides not only a place to live and enjoy but also all of our life-support needs." He died in 2002, when he was eighty-eight years old, and left much of his money to the University of Georgia's ecology program, which was renamed the Odum School.

IN TODAY'S WORLD

Today, scientists and students at the Odum School are working hard to continue his mission to safeguard both the Earth and its inhabitants.

BIODIVERSITY

Use quadrat sampling to study the biodiversity of different ecosystems.

MATERIALS

- 4 sticks, stakes, or dowels
- Measuring tape
- 5 yards (5 m) string or yarn
- Camera or device with a camera
- Notebook
- Plant identification book or app

SAFETY TIPS AND HINTS

Avoid sampling areas near poison ivy and poison oak.

PROTOCOL

1 Choose four ecosystems to sample. For example, you could choose a mowed grass lawn, a mossy bank, a lightly wooded area, a meadow or prairie, a farm field, or an area full of native plants or weeds.

2 Place a stick or stake in the ground at a random spot in one of the ecosystems.

3 Create a quadrat grid in one of the ecosystems by placing four sticks in the ground, 2 yards (2 m) apart, to form a square. (Note: If sampling areas with large trees, you may need to stake out a larger square. Use the same measurements when moving from one ecosystem to another.) *Fig. 1*

4 Tie a string or yarn between the four sticks to enclose the grid. *Fig. 2*

5 When you have created an area of 1 square yard (1 sq m), photograph the square.

Fig. 3: Count the different types of trees, plants, and insects you find inside the square.

6 Count the total number of different types of trees, plants, and insects you find inside the square and record the number in your notebook. As you count, take photos of the plants and animals you find to aid in identification. *Fig. 3*, *Fig. 4*

7 Remove the sticks and string, go to another ecosystem, and repeat the process. *Fig. 5*

8 When you have finished, try to identify what you found and make a list of the total number of different species you found in each grid, even if you can't identify each of them. *Fig. 6*

9 Compare the results from each ecosystem. Are the number of plants and species consistent in each grid? Which ecosystem had the greatest species diversity (most different species)?

10 Think about why some ecosystems are more diverse than others. Did you find less diversity in ecosystems directly exposed to fertilizers and lawn or farm chemicals? Is diversity within an ecosystem important? How does having many tree species in a park, rather than a single species, protect the total number of trees as the climate warms or when there is a disease such as Dutch elm or emerald ash borer?

Fig. I: Create a quadrat grid in one of the ecosystems by placing four sticks in the ground, 2 yards (2 m) apart, to form a square.

Fig. 2: Tie string or yarn between the four stakes to enclose the grid.

Fig. 4: Photograph plants and animals to aid in identification.

Fig. 5: Repeat the process in a different ecosystem.

Fig. 6: Make a list of the species you found in each grid.

CREATIVE ENRICHMENT

Use a sweep net (Lab 13) to get a closer look at insect populations in different ecosystems. For example, compare what you find in prairies to what you find in wooded areas.

THE SCIENCE BEHIND THE FUN

A quadrat is a four-sided figure containing a sample plot. In ecology, quadrat sampling involves marking off a small portion of a larger area so that populations inside of the quadrat can be counted. This type of sampling allows scientists to get an idea of how many plants or animals inhabit a certain area, and the number of each species living there. Quadrat sampling can also be used to study the population of a single species.

Many scientists use inflexible wood or metal grids for this type of sampling. When studying areas with trees, however, flexible grids like the one you use in this lab are more practical. When designing an ecological sampling experiment, ecologists think about what they want to learn and how to best measure organisms within the ecosystem they are interested in. For example, a much larger grid would be required to study giant redwood tree populations than the distribution of moss species.

LAB 12

Akira Miyawaki

(b. 1928)

WEEDS

Akira Miyawaki was born in 1928 in the Okayama Prefecture of Japan, where he grew up watching the people around him clear weeds by hand. As a child in the countryside, he wondered whether there was a way to keep weeds under control without using chemicals. When he completed school, he joined the Tokyo College of Agriculture and Forestry.

A PROFESSOR

While doing fieldwork with his classmates, Akira became fascinated with the variety of plant species in Japan. During holidays at home, he applied his new knowledge to the study of plants and weeds in his village. Although he was told that the study of weeds would never make him famous, he continued in his research and eventually became a professor at Yokohama National University.

VEGETATION MAPPING

After a professor named Dr. Reinhold Tüxen encouraged him to get outdoors and make vegetation maps of the plants he was studying, Akira and his team spent ten years mapping the plant life in Japan. He wrote, "During the day we went out into the field, surveying every different type of plant community in places ranging from forests to grasslands, and even the communities of weeds growing in cities, and at night we compiled and collated our data. This decade was perhaps the most fulfilling period of my life . . . and these data were so important they were practically a census of the nation's greenery." The result of the study was a ten-volume collection of data that is still used today.

SACRED TREES

While exploring Japan, Akira became interested in trees. He noticed that there were old deciduous trees near temples and tombs, while most of the other forests were dominated by needled conifers. Further research told him that the trees near the temples and tombs grew there naturally and had been protected for religious reasons, while conifers had

been introduced to many parts of Japan later. Because trees have many benefits, including protecting soil from being washed away by rain, floods, and tsunamis, Akira wanted to restore natural forests to areas of Japan where trees had been cut down.

THE MIYAWAKI METHOD

Akira visited the forests near trees and temples. He tested the soil where the native trees grew and created a large collection of seeds. Through extensive research, he came up with a method for growing new forests much more quickly than they would grow in the wild. His forest-growing technique was called the "Miyawaki Method." Using this method, a potential forest site is surveyed and the soil is tested. Native seeds are identified, collected, and germinated in a nursery, where the seedlings are pampered until they get strong. Eventually, the seedlings are moved to the area where the forest will be planted and allowed to get used to the new conditions. Finally, the trees are planted close together. Seeds from the new forest are collected when the trees mature.

MILLIONS OF TREES

Dr. Akira Miyawaki tested his forest-planting technique on more than a thousand sites in Japan and helped plant "tiny forests" in cities. He helped people plant more than 40 million native trees and more than 1,700 forests around the world. He even helped the Chinese restore 400,000 trees along the Great Wall of China. In addition to protecting cities, cliffs, and even nuclear power plants from weather events and tsunamis, Akira's forests increase biodiversity, improve soil, and remove enormous volumes of carbon dioxide from the air. In 2006, Akira received the Blue Planet Award for environmental conservation.

IN TODAY'S WORLD

Countries around the world are still using the Miyawaki technique to restore old forests and to plant new ones.

EROSION

Plant chia seeds to learn how trees protect soil from wind and water erosion.

MATERIALS

- Scissors
- 2 empty clear plastic bottles
- Pebbles or small rocks
- Potting soil
- ¼ cup (20 g) chia seeds
- A fork
- Water
- 2 clear bowls, glasses, or jars

SAFETY TIPS AND HINTS

An adult should help young children cut bottles.

Fig. 4: When roots reach the bottom of the planter, pour a cup of water over each planter to compare soil erosion. Catch water in a clear container.

PROTOCOL

1 Use scissors to cut a long hole along one side of each plastic bottle, creating a planter for the chia seeds.

2 Place several pebbles in each planter, near the mouth of the bottle. These will help hold the soil in place. Add dirt to the planter, behind the rocks. The dirt should be 1–1¼ inches (2–3 cm) deep, but the depth can be adjusted, depending on the bottle.

3 Plant chia seeds in one of the planters by evenly sprinkling a few spoonfuls of seed onto the dirt. Use a fork to mix the seeds evenly into the soil and then sprinkle another spoonful of seed over the top of the dirt and mix them into the surface. *Fig. 1*

4 Water the seeds, adding enough water to moisten the dirt entirely. Add the water carefully so that you do not disrupt the dirt. Carefully add water to the other planter, which contains no seeds, to keep the experimental conditions the same for both planters. Water the planters daily, keeping the soil damp but not soaking wet. *Fig. 2*

5 Observe the chia seeds as they sprout. Watch their long roots descend into the soil. *Fig. 3*

6 When the chia plants have grown and the roots reach to the bottom of the container, set the two planters side by side on a flat surface beside two bowls.

7 Holding the chia planter at a slight angle with its mouth over a clear container, pour a cup of water over the plants rapidly, collecting the water that comes out of the bottle. Repeat, using the planter with no chia plants, collecting the water that comes out. *Fig. 4*

8 Compare the water from each planter to see how the roots of plants and trees help hold soil in place, preventing erosion. Consider how plants with long roots might help protect bodies of water such as lakes and streams from substances that can affect the health of ecosystems. *Fig. 5*

Fig. 1: Spread a few spoonfuls of chia seeds into one of the planters. Mix into the soil and sprinkle more seeds on top.

Fig. 2: Add enough water to each planter to moisten the soil. Keep them moist as the seeds sprout and grow.

Fig. 3: Observe the growth of the roots in the planter with chia seeds.

Fig. 5: Compare the soil that drained from each planter.

CREATIVE ENRICHMENT

Make a tree map of trees on your street or in your neighborhood, using a tree identification app if you need to. Note the location, size, and health of the trees and the types of trees you find. Do you find more mature trees or different types of trees near older buildings? Go to your local government website to learn how trees are protected and replaced in your neighborhood.

THE SCIENCE BEHIND THE FUN

Vascular plants have special tissue in their stems to carry water and nutrients. They make up about 80 percent of land plants, including trees, ferns, flowering plants, and grasses. Roots are an important part of vascular plants because they take water and nutrients from the environment and move them into the plant body, helping them grow. Although roots are usually surrounded by soil, the roots of some plants can also grow above ground.

Underground, roots exist in unique ecosystems that scientists are still learning about. Biologists have found evidence that plants can communicate with one another through their roots, using chemical signals. The roots of most plants also have important relationships with fungi.

Tree roots are strong enough to crush and destroy concrete and clog sewer pipes, but they are also strong enough to anchor trees onto slopes and help prevent landslides. Long roots act like chain-link fences in the soil, keeping it in place. Tiny hairs on the roots grip the soil even tighter. They hold plants steady and act like a filter for water passing through. In this lab, you observed that the roots of densely planted chia (*Salvia hispanica*) prevent soil from being washed away by water.

E. O. Wilson

(b. 1929)

AN ACCIDENT

Edward Osborne Wilson was born in Alabama in 1929 and grew up in the southern United States. An only child, he spent hours exploring forests and tide pools. When he was seven, he was in a fishing accident that left him with very little sight in one of his eyes. Luckily, his other eye still worked well, and he used it to focus in on things he could study close-up, such as butterflies and ants.

CITRUS-SCENTED ANTS

Wilson started to collect insects, catching them using nets he made of broom handles, coat hangers, and cheesecloth bags. He became especially fascinated by ants one day when he pulled bark off a rotting tree to expose "short, fat, brilliant yellow" citronella ants that "emitted a strong lemony odor." After reading an article called "Stalking Ants, Savage and Civilized" in *National Geographic* magazine, Edward realized that he could study ants on his own.

AN EAGLE SCOUT

Wilson earned the Eagle Scout award and decided to become an entomologist (a scientist who studies insects). When he was eighteen, he began a survey of all the ants in Alabama and reported the first colony of fire ants ever found in the United States. He earned a B.S. and an M.S. degree from the University of Alabama and transferred to Harvard University to finish his doctorate degree. In 1955, he got his PhD and married Irene Kelley.

THE INSECT SOCIETIES

While at Harvard, Wilson traveled the world, collecting ants in Australia, New Guinea, Fiji, New Caledonia, and Sri Lanka. He often worked with other biologists, ecologists, and even a mathematician to understand more about the diversity of species in ecosystems. He was especially interested in how some insects worked together and how insect societies, such as ant colonies, evolved. Wilson started writing books, using E. O. Wilson as his author name. Soon, his books were famous with both scientists and the public.

A VISIONARY

Wilson's work often challenged traditional ways of thinking about biology and ecology. He wondered whether what he had learned about ants and other insects could be applied to the behavior of other animals, including humans. Although he was at first criticized for his suggestion that human behavior might be related to biology as well as environment, genetic evidence demonstrated that he was correct.

PROTECTING BIODIVERSITY

Wilson was passionate about caring for nature. By studying small islands, he helped develop a mathematical method for studying why different ecosystems contain different numbers of species. He understood that thousands of living organisms, from bacteria and fungi to plants and predators, occupy even the tiniest habitats on Earth. It was painfully obvious that countless species were facing extinction as rain forests were cut down and other rich habits were destroyed by human activity. To address problems he witnessed, Wilson started a biodiversity foundation, wrote books about natural conservation, and spoke passionately about the need for humans to protect wildlife.

IN TODAY'S WORLD

Dr. E. O. Wilson died in 2021, at the age of ninety-two, but his legacy lives on in the work of the people he influenced and the wildlife and forest conservation projects he supported. He said his dream was "that somehow we have as a value, a human value, that we not destroy but we protect and study and understand and love the environment that was our birthplace. And the species that were our birth mates, and the ecosystems that are most able today as they were in the past to take care of themselves, giving us almost infinite benefits . . . I believe that we're on the edge of a new era, in which value is extended to saving the rest of nature. Knowing it, preserving it, studying it, understanding it, cherishing it, and holding on until we know what . . . we're doing."

STUDYING ARTHROPODS

Make a sweep net to capture amazing arthropods.

MATERIALS

- Wire hanger
- Long dowel, broomstick, or sturdy yardstick
- Duct tape
- Stapler (optional)
- Light-colored pillowcase
- Large white piece of light-colored fabric, such as a sheet or tablecloth
- A plastic spoon
- Jars
- Ice cube tray (optional)
- Camera or device with a camera (optional)
- Magnifying glass (optional)
- Notebook (optional)
- Insect identification app or book
- Scissors
- Pliers

SAFETY TIPS AND HINTS

Pillowcases will be damaged, so use old or worn pillowcases for this project.

Use jars to scoop up insects, unless you are sure that they don't bite or sting.

If there are ticks in your area, take precautions and do a tick check after your arthropod hunt.

Fig. 14: Compare invertebrates in different habitats, such as prairie versus marsh or empty lot.

PROTOCOL

1 Bend a wire hanger to form a loop. *Fig. 1*

2 Straighten the wire hook on the end and twist it around the end of a long stick or dowel. *Fig. 2*

3 Tape the hanger snugly onto the long stick or dowel. *Fig. 3*

4 Staple and/or tape the mouth of a pillowcase around the wire loop so that it stays securely on the wire. If you staple, loop the fabric over the hanger, staple together, and tape over the sharp points of the staples. *Fig. 4*, *Fig. 5*

5 Find an area filled with long grass and wildflowers or weeds. Sweep the plants as if sweeping a floor but flip the open side of the net back and forth to capture insects in the grass. *Fig. 6*, *Fig. 7*

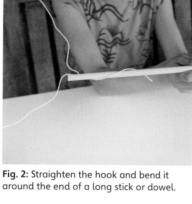

Fig. 1: Bend a wire hanger to form a loop.

Fig. 2: Straighten the hook and bend it around the end of a long stick or dowel.

CREATIVE ENRICHMENT

Sweep sections of the same area at different times of day or in different seasons to see how the population changes.

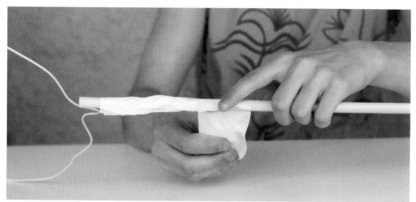

Fig. 3: Tape the hanger snugly to the stick or dowel.

6 Close the net by flipping the bottom over the top. Peek inside to see what you caught. *Fig. 8*

7 Spread a sheet or tablecloth on the ground and carefully shake the insects and arachnids you've collected onto the white fabric. Inspect and photograph them. *Fig. 9*

8 To help contain insects and arachnids and get a closer look, use a plastic spoon to scoop them into jars or an empty ice cube tray. *Fig. 10*, *Fig. 11*

9 Count legs and body segments. Look for antennae. Note wings and unique colors. Use a digital camera or a magnifying glass to get a closer look at each insect and arthropod and record your observations in a notebook. *Fig. 12*, *Fig. 13*

10 Use insect identification apps, books, or other means to identify the organisms you observe. Keep a journal of the insects and arachnids you capture, the time of day, and where you found them. *Fig. 14*

Fig. 4: Staple or tape the mouth of the pillowcase to the wire loop.

project continues ▶

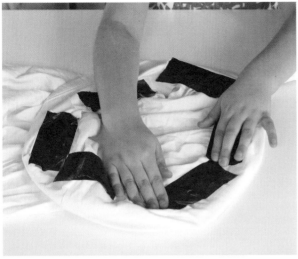

Fig. 5: Cover the staples and gaps with tape.

Fig. 6: Use the net to sweep plants as if sweeping a floor.

Fig. 7: Flip the open side of the net back and forth to capture insects.

Fig. 8: Peek inside to see what you caught.

Fig. 9: Shake the insects and arachnids you've collected onto white fabric.

Fig. 10: Use a plastic spoon to scoop insects and arachnids into an empty ice cube tray.

Fig. I1: Use jars to contain flying insects you catch in the sweep net.

Fig. I2: Count legs and body segments. Look for antennae and note wings and unique colors.

Fig. I3: Insect identification apps can help identify the organisms you capture.

THE SCIENCE BEHIND THE FUN

Arthropods are invertebrates with armor-like skeletons, called exoskeletons, on the outside of their segmented bodies and jointed legs. Insects are arthropods with six legs and sensory organs on their heads called antennae. Insects often have wings, and most grow from egg to larva to adult.

Certain insects, such as butterflies, also go through a pupal stage, in which their bodies are significantly changed before emerging with beautiful wings. Insects can be classified by observation, and insects with similar features are classified into groups, including ants, bees, butterflies, grasshoppers, beetles, and dragonflies.

In this lab, you may also capture some arachnids, which can be identified by their eight jointed legs and hard exoskeletons. Spiders, ticks, and scorpions are all included in this fascinating class of creatures. The bodies of arachnids have only two segments, and they do not have antennae or wings. The pair of legs closest to their head assists them in feeding and self-defense.

C. S. Holling

(b. 1930)

A FOREST

Crawford Stanley Holling, nicknamed "Buzz" by his sister, was born in New York to Canadian parents. He grew up in Canada, surrounded by the trees of Ontario's boreal forest, one of the world's largest intact forests. It is estimated that more than 32,000 insect species inhabit Canada's boreal forest, and it was in those woods where Buzz first developed an interest in insects.

PREDATOR AND PREY

The enormous ecosystem of the forest is inhabited at some time each year by nearly half the birds in North America. It is also home to eighty-five species of mammals, including elk, moose, caribou, grizzly and black bears, wolves, lynx, snowshoe hares, beavers, lemmings, and voles. Exploring the woods and glimpsing insects, birds, and mammals gave Buzz the opportunity to observe predators and prey in their natural habitat. His interest in the predator-prey relationship stayed with him into adulthood.

A THEORY

Buzz studied insects at the University of Toronto and then at the University of British Columbia. For his doctoral dissertation, he developed the first mathematical theory of predation. Called "functional response," it was based on the number of prey in a certain area, how many prey were successfully attacked per predator, and how predators responded to the changing number of prey. Eventually, this theory gave Buzz and other scientists a tool that allowed them to use computer models to study predator-prey relationships in a measurable way. Buzz went to work for the Canadian Department of Forestry and eventually ended up as chair of Ecological Sciences in the Department of Zoology at the University of Florida.

RESILIENCE

In the 1960s and 1970s, Buzz used his theories about the systems of predation to try to learn more about the interactions between humans and nature. Working with other experts, he tried to understand how land, forests, and pest management could be improved, based on what they had learned through their research. Buzz formulated ideas and theories of change, which he called "resilience." For example, a scientist could study the resilience of a system such as a forest. Buzz's research showed him that systems change constantly and that certain disastrous events such as a forest fire or tree disease can yield unexpected results. Sometimes the results are catastrophic and the system collapses, resulting in extinctions. In other cases, systems recover, but some ecological "resources" are redistributed. Later, he applied this idea to human systems.

DIVERSE, DYNAMIC, AND SURPRISING

Buzz called his resilience work the "science of surprise." His work showed him that natural systems are diverse and dynamic. Buzz emphasized that "understanding, rather than knowledge in the narrow sense, is navigating the dynamic, connected, and evolving challenges of our rich, unequal, and beautiful world." He trained many scientists who went on to make major impacts in behavioral ecology, forest management, fisheries, ecology, and sustainability science. Buzz received many honors and awards for his contributions to science and society.

IN TODAY'S WORLD

The mathematical theory and concepts of predation that Dr. C. S. Holling developed in 1957 are still widely used to analyze predator-prey interactions. His theory of functional response (the relationship between prey density and how quickly prey is eaten) is the basis of modern population ecology.

PREDATOR AND PREY PRINTS

Make plaster casts of animal footprints.

MATERIALS

- Cup measures, liquid measuring cups, or metric scale
- Plaster of Paris (gypsum plaster)
- 2 plastic zip-top bags
- Water bottle filled with water
- Camera or device with camera
- Paper towels
- ½ cup (120 ml) measuring cup
- Stick for stirring
- Garden trowel
- Paintbrush or old toothbrush

SAFETY TIPS AND HINTS

Always supervise small children near water.

Sand, sandy soil, and mud work best for casting. It is difficult to cast footprints from clay.

Plaster of Paris hardens quickly, so pour it into footprints immediately after mixing.

PROTOCOL

1 Measure 1 cup (125 g) of plaster of Paris into each of two separate plastic zip-top bags.

2 Fill a bottle with water and put the supplies listed above into a backpack or bag to carry with you.

3 Search for animal footprints in a damp muddy or sandy area, such as a beach or the edge of a pond, lake, or stream. Look for deep footprints with clear borders and take a picture of the tracks and the patterns they make. *Fig. 1*, *Fig. 2*

Fig. 12: Use brushes to gently remove dirt from the plaster footprints.

4 When you've chosen a footprint (or footprints) to cast, use a paper towel to gently remove any standing water without disturbing the impression. *Fig. 3*

5 If you wish, use a stick to dig a circle around the footprint, raising the mud or sand to make sort of a swimming pool to contain the plaster. *Fig. 4*

6 Pour ½ cup (120 ml) of water into one of the plastic bags containing the plaster of Paris. Mix well by kneading the bag and stirring with the stick, if needed. Once mixed, it will harden in 4–6 minutes. *Fig. 5*, *Fig. 6*

7 Immediately pour the plaster of Paris into each footprint. Fill the print first, and then the "swimming pool" area. Use a stick to smooth it out on top and when it starts to dry, use a stick to scratch the date onto the plaster. *Fig. 7*

8 After 15 minutes, use the trowel to dig around the plaster so that the sides can dry. *Fig. 8*

9 Wait 30 minutes and then check the plaster to see if it is solid. Plaster loses its shine and looks dull when it has hardened. Carefully dig the cast out, along with a few inches of the sand and mud around it so that it does not break. Let it dry overnight. *Fig. 9*, *Fig. 10*, *Fig. 11*

10 When the cast is completely dry, use your fingers and then a toothbrush or paintbrush to remove the dirt on the cast. *Fig. 12*

11 Try to identify the footprints you cast. *Fig. 13*

Fig. I: Search for animal footprints in a damp muddy or sandy area.

Fig. 2: Look for deep footprints with clear edges.

CREATIVE ENRICHMENT

See how many types of footprints you can cast from a single area to get an idea of what animals live in that ecosystem. Which are predators and which are prey?

project continues ▶

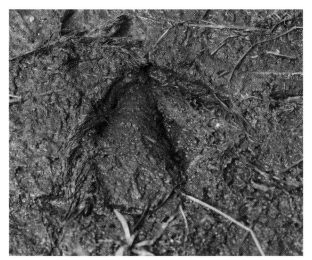
Fig. 3: Use a paper towel to remove any standing water in the footprints.

Fig. 4: A stick can be used to dig a trench around the footprint.

Fig. 5: Pour ½ cup (120 ml) of water into the I cup (125 g) plaster of Paris.

Fig. 6: Mix the water and plaster of Paris together until smooth.

Fig. 7: Pour liquid plaster of Paris into the footprints.

Fig. 8: After I5 minutes, dig a deep trough around the footprint.

Fig. 9: After around 30 minutes, or when the plaster of Paris feels solid, carefully dig the footprints out of the mud.

Fig. 10: As it dries, the plaster loses its shine and looks dull.

Fig. 11: Let the plaster dry overnight.

Fig. 13: Count the number of toes in each footprint and try to identify the animal that made it.

THE SCIENCE BEHIND THE FUN

Animal tracks are clues to more than just foot size. They tell us how animals move, where they gather, and even how long their strides are. Fossilized dinosaur footprints, for example, are signatures of animals that walked the Earth millions of years ago. They reveal secrets about dinosaur behavior that bones alone can't illuminate.

To identify animal tracks, it is important to make certain observations and ask the right questions. When looking at mammal tracks, for example, always count the toes. Canines (dogs), felines (cats), and rabbits all show four toes on front and hind leg tracks. Other animals, such as rodents, show four toes on the front feet and five toes on the back. It can be tricky to tell the difference between front and back feet.

Notice whether toe prints show round pads or long fingers, like those of a raccoon. Look for claws, which usually show up on canine tracks and bear tracks. Observe the shape of the palm pad. Is there just one, or are there several? Most cats, dogs, and raccoons have a single palm pad. When looking at bird footprints, look for webbing between the toes.

LAB 15

O'Neil Ray Collins

(b. 1931)

A UNIQUE PERSPECTIVE

The eighth of nine children, O'Neil Ray Collins was born in 1931 in Plaisance, Louisiana. He went by the name Ray, and his parents were cotton farmers. Later in life, he told friends and colleagues about growing up in the South and the racism he and his family faced. When he was young, only light-skinned partygoers would be allowed into dances. Some of his relatives had attempted to "pass" for white to have a better life, which tragically cut them off from their families. Throughout his life, Ray was passionate about sharing these experiences to illustrate that the challenges he'd faced gave him a different and important perspective on the world.

PUFFBALLS AND YEAST

In 1948, Ray graduated from high school, joined the army, and then went to college, where he earned a degree in botany. He was the first in his family to graduate from college, and it was at Southern University where he first encountered mycology (the study of fungi). However, he'd been interested in fungi since childhood; he recalled finding huge white puffballs on the ground in Louisiana, and the clouds of brown spores that exploded out when they were hit with a stick. Ray also remembered the yeast his mother would use to make bread dough rise.

A MENTOR

Lafayette Frederick, a Black botany professor at Southern University, had introduced Ray to mycology and encouraged him to go to graduate school. At that time, the University of Iowa was a center for mycology, and Ray received his master's degree from Iowa and then his PhD, in 1961. While in graduate school, Ray met his wife, Ann Walker, who was studying speech and drama. He always said that it was Ann's belief in him that gave him courage, early in his career, to apply for academic positions outside of the South.

CREEPING SLIME

Ray was interested in studying fascinating organisms called plasmodial slime molds. Slime molds are life-forms that can live as single cells. However, when conditions are right, the cells clump together, reproduce, and can sometimes crawl across surfaces as a single, gelatinous blob. Ray was especially interested in how certain slime molds reproduce, and he made several important discoveries in slime mold genetics. In addition to his research, Ray was a very good teacher, with a big baritone voice. Students recall him waving his hands and saying, "I was really excited when I learned this."

WORKING FOR OTHERS

Dr. O'Neil Ray Collins continued to do research while he worked as an instructor and professor at several colleges and universities. In 1969, he accepted a full professorship at the University of California, Berkeley. The only tenured Black professor at Berkeley, he was one of only a few visible Black biologists in the United States. In addition to his research and teaching, Ray worked hard to increase diversity at the university. Under his leadership, the school's graduate division developed the Graduate Minority Program, which helped underrepresented students enter and succeed in all departments. From 1976 to 1981, Ray served as chairman of the Department of Botany, and during his tenure at Berkeley, he received several important awards for his accomplishments in the field of mycology. He and his wife were also members of a faculty drama club, where Ray had several leading roles. He died in 1989.

IN TODAY'S WORLD

Currently, researchers are studying slime molds to learn more about human brain development. Scientists and engineers creating bio-based computing systems by studying ant colonies are also looking to slime molds for inspiration.

DISSECT A MUSHROOM

Dissect a mushroom
and make prints from
the spores.

MATERIALS

- Whole white button mushrooms (closed mushrooms work best)
- Several types of mushrooms from the grocery store (optional)
- Magnifying glass
- Sharp knife
- Drawing paper
- Colored pencils, crayons, or markers
- Heavy white paper
- Baking sheet
- Water
- Bowls or other containers to cover mushrooms
- Aerosol hairspray (optional)

Fig. 2: Use a magnifying glass for a closer look.

SAFETY TIPS AND HINTS

Never eat wild mushrooms unless an expert identifies them as edible. Many mushroom species are poisonous.

For small children, parental supervision is recommended for the cutting step.

PROTOCOL

1 Examine different types of mushrooms under a magnifying glass. Cut them lengthwise and in cross-sections to observe the structure. *Fig. 1*, *Fig. 2*

2 On drawing paper and using colored pencils or crayons, illustrate the mushrooms, including stems, caps, and gills. Draw cross-sections of the mushrooms you cut. *Fig. 3*

3 Lay a few pieces of heavy white paper on a baking sheet.

4 Cut the stems and bottoms off some button mushrooms so that the "gills" are exposed. *Fig. 4*

5 Place the mushrooms, gill-side down, on the white paper. Put a drop of water on top of each mushroom cap and cover the mushrooms with a bowl or another container. *Fig. 5*

6 Find a dark spot for the baking sheet and leave the mushrooms in the dark for 24 hours.

7 After 24 hours, remove the bowls from the mushrooms to see whether the spores have fallen from the gills onto the paper to leave a print. *Fig. 6*

8 When you have prints, remove the mushrooms from the paper and let the paper dry.

9 If you have different types of edible mushrooms, repeat the experiment and compare spore patterns to see how they vary between species. *Fig. 7*

10 (Optional) Use aerosol hairspray to fix the spores to the paper.

CREATIVE ENRICHMENT

Go on a hunt for wild mushrooms and other fungi. Look for fungi on trees, rotting wood, the forest floor, and in lawns and gardens. Try to identify the mushrooms you photograph.

Fig. 1: Gather mushrooms to study and cut them into cross-sections.

Fig. 3: Draw the mushrooms, including details such as gills.

Fig. 4: Cut the bottom and stems from button mushrooms to expose the gills.

Fig. 5: Place the mushrooms, gill-side down, on smooth, heavy white paper and cover with cups or bowls.

Fig. 6: After 24 hours, remove the mushrooms to reveal spore prints.

Fig. 7: Compare spore prints from different types of mushrooms.

THE SCIENCE BEHIND THE FUN

Fungi (fun-guy) such as molds, yeast, and mushrooms are more closely related to humans than to plants. They are essential to Earth's ecosystems because they are saprophytes (sap-ruh-fights), which means that they eat dead things. Expert recyclers, fungi aid in the decomposition of manure and rotting plants and animals. By releasing the chemicals bound up in organic matter, they release nutrients for use by other living organisms.

Certain fungi, called mycorrhizal fungi, have a symbiotic partnership with plants, which means that they depend on one another for survival. This relationship is essential for farm, prairie, and forest alike, and without fungi, most grasses and trees would not survive.

Mushrooms are the "fruiting body" of fungal organisms called basidiomycetes (bass-ih-dee-oh-my-seats). Basidiomycetes have three parts: the aboveground mushrooms, root-like mycelium (my-silly-um) that break down decomposing matter, and spores. Spores, which fall onto paper to create the "mushroom prints" in this lab, are the reproductive cells of mushrooms.

Sylvia Earle

(b. 1935)

POND EXPLORER

The ocean first got American oceanographer Sylvia Earle's attention when she was three years old and a wave knocked her off her feet. She's been running back into the water ever since. Born in 1935, Sylvia lived on a farm in New Jersey with her parents and two brothers until she was thirteen. A nature lover, she spent her free time exploring the life in their backyard pond, catching fish and tadpoles to keep in jars where she could observe them more closely. When her family moved to Florida, her interest immediately shifted to the wildlife in the Gulf of Mexico.

SCUBA

Sylvia was such a dedicated student that she graduated from high school when she was sixteen and got a scholarship to Florida State University. Interested in marine plants, she became a certified SCUBA diver to study her subjects close-up. Sylvia went to graduate school at Duke University and focused her research on plants called algae, which live in the water and turn carbon dioxide and sunlight into oxygen and sugars. After pausing her education to have two children, she completed her PhD in botany (the study of plants), collecting more than 20,000 samples of algae from the Gulf of Mexico. She was one of the first biologists to use SCUBA to document ocean organisms.

LIFE UNDER WATER

It was unusual for women to join ocean research expeditions at that time, but Sylvia joined several, accompanying research crews on voyages to the Galápagos Islands, the Chilean coast, and the Panama Canal Zone. She did all this while raising two children, taking classes, and writing her PhD dissertation. Sylvia continued to dive on expeditions around the world and was the first woman to set foot in an underwater habitat where scientists could live 100 feet (30.5 m) below the surface. In 1970, she led an all-female team to live and dive 50 feet (15 m) under water in the Tektite II Project, near the U.S. Virgin Islands.

A DEEP DIVE

Sylvia dove with sperm whales for the 1980 film *Gentle Giants of the Pacific*. In 1979, she famously rode a submarine to the ocean floor off the coast of Hawaii. Wearing a pressurized "JIM" suit, she was carried down 1,250 feet (381 m), deeper than anyone has ever walked the ocean floor untethered. Detaching from the submarine, she walked along the bottom for two and a half hours. Far from the sun's light, the water was inky black and she was surrounded by glowing bioluminescent creatures. Sylvia said that the experience was like diving into a galaxy of lights.

NOAA

Sylvia was the first woman to be chief scientist of the U.S. National Ocean and Atmospheric Administration (NOAA). In 1998, she was named *Time* magazine's first Hero for the Planet. Passionate about protecting the ocean, Sylvia wants people to understand how important it is to all of us. She says, "You should treat the ocean as if your life depended on it, because it does!" and reminds people that "with every breath they take, with every drop of water they drink, the ocean is touching them."

IN TODAY'S WORLD

Dr. Sylvia Earle continues to educate the public about our oceans and leads Mission Blue, which is working to inspire "an upwelling of public awareness, access and support for a worldwide network of marine protected areas."

OCEAN CLEANUP

Create an oil spill in a bowl and try to clean it up.

MATERIALS

- 2 clear bowls
- Water
- Rimmed baking sheet or tray
- Blue food coloring
- Vegetable, corn, canola, or olive oil
- Feathers
- Dish soap
- Spoon
- Cotton balls, paper towels, polyester cloth, and other fabric scraps
- Sunscreen

SAFETY TIPS AND HINTS

Do this project on a rimmed baking sheet or outdoors to minimize the mess.

Fig. 3: Dip a feather into the oily water.

PROTOCOL

1 Fill two clear bowls with water and set them on a baking sheet or tray. Put a few drops of food coloring into one of the bowls. *Fig. 1*

2 Add oil to the blue water so that it completely covers the surface to represent an oil spill in the ocean. (Oil is less dense than water, so it will float on top.) *Fig. 2*

3 Put a feather in the bowl and then remove it. Observe how the feather changes when it is coated with oil. *Fig. 3*, *Fig. 4*

4 Try to rinse the oil off the feather using only water.

5 Use dish detergent to remove oil from the feather. *Fig. 5*

6 Attempt to remove the oil from the water in the bowl using a spoon, cotton balls, paper towels, and other materials to see what absorbs oil best. *Fig. 6*

7 To see how sunscreen moves from human skin to coral reefs, apply a generous amount of sunscreen to one of your hands.

8 Imagine that you are swimming in the ocean and put your hand into the bowl of clean water. Chances are, you will see some of the sunscreen move into the water. Using reef-safe sunscreen (sunscreen without oxybenzone and octinoxate) can help prevent damage to ocean ecosystems. *Fig. 7*

CREATIVE ENRICHMENT

Using what you learned, come up with an idea for cleaning up a large oil spill in the ocean.

Fig. 1: Add a few drops of food coloring to a bowl of water.

Fig. 2: Pour oil onto the surface of the water to represent an oil spill.

Fig. 4: Observe how a feather changes when covered with oil.

Fig. 5: Use dish detergent to wash the feather.

Fig. 6: Use different materials to try to remove the oil from the water.

Fig. 7: Apply sunscreen to your hand and dip it in water to see how chemicals move from your skin to the water.

THE SCIENCE BEHIND THE FUN

Imagine the environmental damage that occurs when oil tankers or undersea oil wells spring a leak. Hundreds of thousands of gallons of oil can spill into the ocean in a single day. In this lab, you see how oil clings to feathers and doesn't come off with water. Imagine the effect of an oil spill on ocean birds.

Synthetic fabrics such as polyester are made from petroleum products, which contain lots of carbon and hydrogen atoms. Carbon and hydrogen are the same chemical elements found in oil, and oil is attracted to

polyester. Polypropylene, another synthetic material made from carbon and hydrogen that floats on water, also attracts oil and is often used in cleaning up oil spills.

While it's up to government officials and companies to make rules so that oil tankers and wells don't leak, you can protect ocean animals too. Certain sunscreens contain chemicals such as oxybenzone and octinoxate, which can harm animals that live in the water. By choosing mineral sunscreens without these chemicals, you protect both your skin and marine ecosystems.

Wangari Maathai

(b. 1940)

KIKUYU KNOWLEDGE

Wangari Maathai was born in 1940 and grew up in the Kikuyu community in the central highlands of Kenya, surrounded by natural beauty in the countryside. She recalled her mother telling her not to collect firewood from fig trees, which were sacred to their people. When she got older, Wangari realized that those special trees protected the sloping landscape.

A DOCTORATE DEGREE

After attending primary school in Kenya, Wangari went to Mount St. Scholastic College in Kansas, where she majored in biology. Next, she earned a master's degree in biology from the University of Pittsburgh, in Pennsylvania. Returning to Africa, she attended the University of Nairobi and became the first woman in East Africa to earn a doctorate degree.

A CHANGED LANDSCAPE

While in the United States, Wangari was greatly influenced by the civil rights movement, and in graduate school she became a member of the National Council of Women. At one of their meetings, she learned what was happening to the environment in her beloved Kenya, which had changed dramatically over the five years when she was in America. After gaining independence from British rule, Kenya's newly independent government embraced commercial agriculture, cutting down trees to plant cash crops and build new housing developments.

DESERTIFICATION

Trees had been cut down, streams had been drying up, the water was polluted, and harvests had not been good. Women had to walk long distances to find firewood for cooking and boiling water and worried about feeding their families. Wangari understood that trees hold soil and water in place after it rains. She recognized that many of the problems in her country were the direct result of deforestation. Agriculture and development were turning fertile land into desert.

THE GREEN BELT MOVEMENT

To help solve the environmental problems, Wangari helped found the Green Belt Movement, which promised to plant millions of trees throughout Kenya. She understood that planting trees would help restore ecosystems and provide food and fuel for communities. She also fought against cutting down more forest for building and housing developments. Much of the deforestation had been done illegally, with the blessing of a corrupt government. Wangari was threatened, beaten, and even sent to jail for standing up to the men in charge, but she never gave up and mobilized thousands of women and men to plant trees. Eventually, the government changed and things got better.

52 MILLION NEW TREES

Through the simple act of planting trees, Wangari was helping to solve a very complicated problem. She understood that ecology is more than a scientific discipline. It is a matter of war, peace, human rights, and the survival of species, including ours. In 2004, she was awarded the Nobel Peace Prize. The Green Belt Movement has already planted more than 52 million trees. Wangari died in 2011.

GREEN LIFE

In a 2006 radio interview, Dr. Wangari Maathai said, "We want to do whatever it takes to ensure that we do not eliminate ourselves from this planet by exploiting the resources we need . . . green life is the only life that is able to trap the sun's energy and give us food and clean the air that we breathe. So we know, therefore, that we must maintain the green life on this planet. And that if we were to desertify this planet and remove every green vegetation, we would be dead before the last tree dies."

IN TODAY'S WORLD

Trees are very efficient at removing carbon dioxide from the atmosphere. With climate change, it is now more important than ever that we stop deforestation and plant trees to replace those that have been cut down.

GERMINATION IN A JAR

Germinate beans in a jar and plant a tree.

MATERIALS

- Paper towels
- Wide-mouth jar
- Water (preferably tap water)
- Seeds from a tree, such as a maple tree (optional)
- Dried beans
- Plastic wrap
- Notebook
- Paper and colored pencils
- Camera or device with a camera (optional)
- Magnifying glass
- Small pot with soil

SAFETY TIPS AND HINTS

Be sure to use beans that haven't been precooked.

Fig. 5: Observe the seeds as they sprout and grow.

PROTOCOL

1 Fold a paper towel in half or in thirds so that it is the same height as a wide-mouth jar. Roll the paper towel so that it fits into the jar and is snug against the interior. *Fig. 1*

2 Add some water to the jar and roll the jar until the entire paper towel is wet. *Fig. 2*

3 Pour out excess water and then arrange the paper towel so that it is tight against the inside of the jar. *Fig. 3*

4 Push some seeds or beans into the jar, between the paper towel and the glass so that they are approximately halfway down the wall of the jar. *Fig. 4*

5 Use a small piece of plastic wrap to lightly cover the mouth of the jar. Put the jar in a sunny spot and check the paper every day to make sure that it is damp. Add water as needed.

6 Observe germination as the seeds begin to send out roots, sprouts, and leaves. Use a notebook to record your observations. Draw what you see or take pictures. Use a magnifying glass to see more details. *Fig. 5*

7 When the seeds or beans have a few leaves, you can transplant them into a small pot of soil. Keep the soil damp and allow the seedlings to grow and get stronger. *Fig. 6*

8 Search for maple seeds (see *Fig. 6*) and use them to plant a maple tree in a pot or in the ground. Water the seed regularly and when the seedling is big enough, transplant it. If you are planting a tree, think about how large it will be someday and find a spot with space for it to grow. *Fig. 7*, *Fig. 8*, *Fig. 9*, *Fig. 10*, *Fig. 11*

Fig. 1: Fold a paper towel and roll it to fit into a jar.

Fig. 2: Pour some water into the jar to wet the paper towel.

Fig. 3: Pour out excess water.

Fig. 4: Place beans or tree seeds between the paper towel and the glass.

project continues ▶

Fig. 6: Watch as leaves emerge. When plants are large enough, transplant them to a pot or into the ground.

Fig. 7: Look for maple seeds or other tree seeds.

Fig. 8: Maple trees are found in Asia, Europe, and North America.

Fig. 9: Plant a maple seed.

Fig. I0: Keep the soil damp while the seed sprouts and grows.

CREATIVE ENRICHMENT

Visit a plant nursery or tree farm to learn more about which trees grow best in your area. Look for opportunities to help plant trees in your neighborhood, or start an environmental club at your school with the goal of planting more trees. Cities often have opportunities for residents to help plant seedlings in local parks. Always call the power company before digging to plant a tree, in case there is a buried power line.

Fig. II: When it has several leaves, transplant the tree into the ground.

THE SCIENCE BEHIND THE FUN

Seeds are packages containing dormant (sleeping) embryonic plants, along with all of the nutrients a plant needs to start growing. Dormant plants wait for certain signals before germinating. They need water, sunlight, air, and often a certain temperature before they send out roots, sprout, and grow leaves.

At first, sprouts get their nutrients from the seed they grew from, and in this lab you may notice seeds shrinking as plants get bigger. Eventually, most plants require the nutrients found in soil to continue growing. Transplanting the seedling you grow in this lab allows them to stretch their roots to find water and stretch their leaves to the sun.

Plants use a chemical process called photosynthesis to transform the sun's energy, water, and carbon dioxide gas from the atmosphere into chemical energy and oxygen. Some of the chemical energy in plants is stored as carbohydrates like sugars and starches. This locks carbon from atmospheric carbon dioxide inside the plant, until it dies and decomposes (breaks down) or is burned.

Wangari Maathai recognized that tree roots hold soil in place and prevent it from being washed away by water or blown away by the wind. Planting trees and preventing mature trees from being cut down preserves existing ecosystems and creates new ones where microorganisms, invertebrates, and animals can live. Trees also help with the problem of climate change by pulling carbon dioxide out of the air and locking it in their trunks and branches.

Robin Wall Kimmerer

(b. 1953)

THE HEART BERRY

Born in 1953, Robin Wall Kimmerer grew up in Upstate New York. In English, her Potawatomi name means "Light Shining through Sky Woman." The Potawatomi Nation originally lived in the Great Lakes region of the United States but in the late 1700s, many Potawatomi were forcibly removed by the government to a reservation in Oklahoma. It was nature that helped Robin and her parents reconnect with their Potawatomi heritage. As a girl, she loved exploring the fields and woods and wrote that "it was the wild strawberries, beneath dewy leaves on an almost-summer morning, who gave me my sense of the world, my place in it." According to Robin, "In Potawatomi, the strawberry is 'ode min,' the heart berry. We recognize them as the leaders of the berries, the first to bear fruit."

MOSS

Robin earned a master's degree in botany and then a PhD in plant ecology from the University of Wisconsin, Madison. While studying forest ecology in graduate school, she became fascinated by mosses, which are small plants with no roots. Studying them close-up, she discovered an entire miniature world. After teaching in Kentucky, Robin moved back to Upstate New York to become a professor at State University of New York College of Environmental Science and Forestry (ESF), where she had received her bachelor's degree.

WAYS OF KNOWING

Today, Robin is interested in educating her students and the public about science and traditional ecological knowledge. She wrote an award-winning book called *Gathering Moss: A Natural and Culture History of Mosses*, which beautifully weaves plant ecology into Robin's understanding of traditional knowledge, or "ways of knowing." Robin is also the director of the Center for Native Peoples and the Environment at ESF. The program gives Indigenous students more opportunities to study environmental science and allows traditional science to benefit from the wisdom of Native philosophy. Robin hopes that the center will help us reach the common goal of sustainability.

WORDS MATTER

Dr. Robin Wall Kimmerer thinks that language is extremely important. As a writer and a scientist, she is interested in "not only the restoration of ecological communities, but restoration of our relationships to land." She believes that our words affect our behavior and our attitude about the world. Rather than referring to the Earth as a thing, or "it," she suggests that we refer to our planet and everything natural thing on it as family, or "kin." She hopes that once we stop seeing nature as separate from ourselves, we will take better care of our world. Robin is also learning the Potawatomi language.

A MOTHER, A SCIENTIST, A WRITER, AND A MEMBER OF A FIRST NATION

Grateful for all the gifts that the Earth has given her, Robin writes, "Knowing that you love the Earth changes you, activates you to protect and defend and celebrate. But when you feel that the Earth loves you in return, that feeling transforms the relationship from a one-way street into a sacred bond." Her identity as a mother, a scientist, a writer, and a member of a First Nation has made her a social activist for the environment, sustainability, social justice, and Native American issues. Dr. Robin Wall Kimmerer's award-winning book, *Braiding Sweetgrass*, beautifully illustrates the interdependence of humans and the natural world.

OBSERVING MOSS CLOSE-UP

Take a closer look at moss. Collect small clumps of moss to cultivate at home.

MATERIALS

- Camera or device with camera (optional)
- Magnifying glass
- Garden trowel or small shovel
- Notebook
- Bags or containers for carrying moss
- Large flat container or terrarium container
- Small rocks or pebbles
- Water
- Spray bottle
- Microscope (optional)
- Petri dish or glass slide and cover (optional)

SAFETY TIPS AND HINTS

Do not collect mosses from protected areas, such as national and state parks. Always ask permission before collecting moss on private property.

Moss grows very slowly and can take years to regrow once disturbed. Take only small patches of moss if you want to cultivate some at home.

PROTOCOL

1 Go on a moss hunt. Look for velvety green masses in yards, woods, and on rocks. Mosses like damp, shady habitats and can grow on dirt, rocks, gravel, rotting wood, and even concrete.

2 Photograph moss and moss-like plants you discover. Get close to the moss you find and observe it from eye level and through a magnifying glass. *Fig. 1*, *Fig. 2*

Fig. 2: Study the moss at eye level, to see all the structures close-up.

3 With a garden trowel, take small samples of the moss you find, removing it along with some of the substrate (soil, sand, or wood) it is growing on. Record the origin of each sample collected in your science notebook. *Fig. 3*, *Fig. 4*

4 Place the moss in a container to bring it home.

5 Make a moss terrarium. Fill a container with small rocks. *Fig. 5*

6 Add water to the container so that it comes just to the top of the rocks. Place the moss samples on top of the rocks. *Fig. 6*

7 With a spray bottle of water, mist the moss regularly and water the base of the rocks as needed. *Fig. 7*, *Fig. 8*

8 Observe changes in the mosses as they grow indoors. Consider how conditions in the terrarium are different from conditions in the ecosystem where you collected the moss.

Fig. 1: Observe moss through a magnifying glass.

Fig. 3: Gently remove a small patch of moss, along with the material it is growing on.

Fig. 4: Try to collect several different types of mosses.

Fig. 5: Add small rocks to the bottom of a clear container.

project continues ▶

OBSERVING MOSS CLOSE-UP 91

CREATIVE ENRICHMENT

1 Use a microscope to study and compare different types of moss. *Fig. 1*, *Fig. 2*, *Fig. 3*

2 To look for living organisms such as worms and tardigrades, cover moss with bottled water in a separate dish. Let it sit for several minutes.

3 Squeeze the excess water from the moss onto a small plate. Place a drop of the moss water onto a microscope slide and add a cover slip. *Fig. 4*

4 Observe the sample under a microscope, starting with the lowest power to search for movement and then increasing magnification. *Fig. 5*, *Fig. 6*

Fig. 1: Use a microscope to magnify the moss.

Fig. 2: Compare different mosses and their structures.

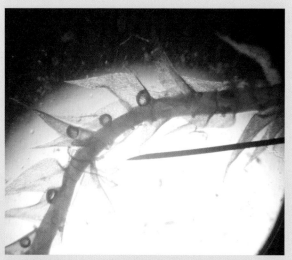

Fig. 3: Moss leaves are often made up of a single layer of cells.

Fig. 4: Soak moss in bottled water, squeeze water from the moss, and observe it under a microscope.

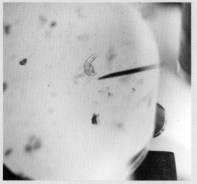

Fig. 5: Look for movement to find living organisms like this one.

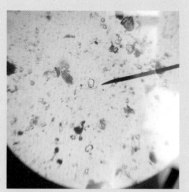

Fig. 6: Common moss dwellers include worms called nematodes.

Fig. 6: Add water to the rocks and place moss samples on the rocks.

Fig. 7: Mist the moss with water.

Fig. 8: Keep the container covered and mist the moss with water occasionally. Observe how it changes.

THE SCIENCE BEHIND THE FUN

Mosses, which often form dense green mats on forest floors and damp, shady surfaces, are nonflowering plants. Called bryophytes (bry-yo-fights), they have stems and leaves, but mosses don't have true roots. Important inhabitants of many ecosystems, they stabilize the surface of soil and hold water in, helping new plants grow. When an area is affected by forest fires or deforestation, mosses are among the first plants to move back in to help heal the land.

Often found in rainy or foggy areas, mosses lack structures for carrying water and must absorb moisture directly from the environment to survive. Different moss species require different conditions to grow. Because they hate competition, moss is often found growing where other organisms don't thrive, such as on rocks, packed soil, or wood. Anchored to surfaces by structures called rhizoids, some mosses love the sun, while others hide in caves.

Mosses play home to a zoo of living organisms. A few of the water-loving invertebrates commonly found in the film of water on mosses are tardigrades, nematodes (worms), and rotifers. All are very small, but they can be observed wiggling under the lens of a microscope.

Rodrigo A. Medellín

(b. 1957)

A CONTEST

Rodrigo Medellín was born in 1957 in Mexico City. The youngest of five, Rodrigo loved animals. When he was eleven, he became the first kid to compete in a national contest for adults by answering questions about mammals. He became popular on TV, and when he was thirteen, Rodrigo had the opportunity to hold a bat in his hand. The experience made him feel "awe, admiration, and curiosity," he said. Rodrigo had very patient parents who allowed him to bring animals home to study, including vampire bats. A vampire bat eats only about 2 teaspoons (10 ml) of blood per night, and Rodrigo fed his bats blood from live cows at a nearby vet school, which he froze in ice cube trays.

A BAD REPUTATION

Rodrigo thinks that bats mostly got their bad reputation because of vampire bats. According to him, out of more than 1,400 species of bats in the world, only three feed on blood. He explains that when the Spanish explorer Cortés came to Mexico in the 1500s, some of his men noticed bats licking blood from the shoulders of their horses and wrote about it. Then, in the 1890s, the famous author Bram Stoker heard about Mexico's blood-sucking bats and wrote in the novel *Dracula* that his vampire moved around by turning into a bat.

BAT MAN OF MEXICO

In 1986, Rodrigo got a degree in biology from the University of Mexico, where he is now a senior professor of ecology. He earned a PhD at the University of Florida, studying community ecology and conservation of mammals. Rodrigo is well known for his work on bat, jaguar, and bighorn sheep conservation. Because many people are afraid of bats and think of them only as disease carriers, Rodrigo, called the Bat Man of Mexico, has devoted his life to changing their image. He likes to point out that birds carry more diseases than bats do and that bats are essential for pollinating plants and spreading seeds. Teaching farmers about the benefits of bats is particularly important. For example, by putting bat houses in rice fields, scientists have observed a 60 percent decrease in pests.

SAVED FROM EXTINCTION

Blue agave plants, which are used to make the Mexican liquor tequila, are pollinated by lesser long-nosed bats, but farmers had started removing the flowers from agave plants to increase their sugar content. This practice threatened the bats, which feed on the flowers. Rodrigo and his team explained the importance of the bats to the agave farmers, who stopped removing the flowers. Today, the population of lesser long-nosed bats has recovered and they have come off the endangered species list.

BAT HOUSES

Dr. Rodrigo Medellín is a well-known science communicator and has given lectures all around the world. He reminds us not to be afraid of bats and suggests putting up bat houses. Though he kept bats as a teenager, Rodrigo knows that they can carry some diseases, including rabies, so people should never touch live or dead bats in the wild or in their houses.

IN TODAY'S WORLD

Today, Rodrigo continues to study the travel patterns of bats and how they communicate using echolocation (location using reflected sound). GPS technology is now allowing him to study the migration of reproducing female bats.

ECHOLOCATION

Do an echolocation experiment to see how bats locate their prey.

MATERIALS

- **2 cardboard tubes, around 10 inches (25 cm) long, or construction paper**
- **Tape**
- **Metal baking sheet**

SAFETY TIPS AND HINTS

Two people are required to do this experiment.

PROTOCOL

1 Stand several feet away from a window, close your eyes, and say "hello." Keeping your eyes closed, take a step forward and say hello again in the same tone and volume. Carefully, repeat until your mouth is almost against the window and then back away again, saying "hello." Try it again to see whether the sound changes as you approach the window and retreat from it. *Fig. 1*, *Fig. 2*

2 Do an experiment to see how sound waves bounce off solid objects. You will need two people. One person, the "bat," will produce the sound waves. The second person will listen for the echo of the sound the first person produced.

3 If you don't have two cardboard tubes, make tubes by rolling and taping paper.

4 Set a metal baking sheet up against a wall so that it is almost vertical. It will act as a surface for reflecting sound waves.

Fig. 3: The "bat" will whisper a word through the cardboard tube, and the "listener" will try to hear what they say.

5 Sound waves bounce off hard surfaces and are reflected back at the same angle that they hit. The "bat" should position their tube at about a 45-degree angle, at least 12 inches (30 cm) from the baking sheet, and put their mouth to the tube.

6 The listener should hold the other tube at a 45-degree angle opposite the "bat," with their ear to the tube. The "bat" will whisper a word through the cardboard tube, and the listener will try to hear what they said, as sound waves bounce off the baking sheet. *Fig. 3*

CREATIVE ENRICHMENT

Blindfold the "bat." Have the second person move around the room, occasionally making a sound. The bat should point where they think the person is. Have the "bat" plug one ear and repeat the experiment to see how two ears make it easier to locate an object using sound.

Fig. I: Stand several feet away from a window, close your eyes, and say "hello."

Fig. 2: Test whether the sound changes as you approach the window.

THE SCIENCE BEHIND THE FUN

When objects vibrate in the air, air molecules are squashed together to create repeating pressure waves called sound. Water molecules can also carry sound waves. Many animals, including bats and dolphins, use sound waves to get information about their environment.

Echolocation is a word used to describe how these animals use sound to "see" other objects such as prey when visibility is low, such as in the dark or underwater. Bats make high-frequency squeaks and clicks, which are composed of fast sound wave vibrations. When these sound waves hit objects, they are reflected and bounce back to the animal that made them.

The ears of bats have evolved to be very sensitive to sound waves. They are fine-tuned to their own calls, and having two ears helps them triangulate the location of objects. This helps them navigate, predict the size of objects, and chase fast-moving insects.

LAB 20

Dana Bergstrom

(b. 1962)

NATURE LOVER

Born in Sydney, Australia, Dana Bergstrom knew she wanted to be scientist when she was five years old. After school, she'd climb trees and create miniature African landscapes populated with plastic lions and elephants. Sometimes, Dana's mom took her and her sister to Manly Beach to explore tide pools. Dana also loved pouring over the photographs in *National Geographic* and an atlas of the world, which contained drawings of plants, minerals, and dinosaurs.

A WOMAN IN THE FIELD

By the time she was twelve, Dana knew that she wanted to be an ecologist. After high school, she pursued her dream of becoming an ecologist by completing undergraduate and graduate degrees at Macquarie University. At that time, there were mostly men in the Australian Antarctic program, but she forged a new path as one of the first female scientists to travel south to do fieldwork over a long period of time.

AN ENDANGERED ECOSYSTEM

To do research for her master's degree and PhD, Dana traveled to Macquarie Island in the southwestern Pacific Ocean. About halfway between New Zealand and Antarctica, it is one of the cloudiest places on Earth. Part of the Antipodes Subantarctic Islands tundra ecoregion, Macquarie Island is home to the world's entire royal penguin population during their annual nesting season and has an interesting ecological history. Dana was focused on studying unique vegetation on the island, but while she was there, other native species were struggling for survival due to invasive rats, cats, and rabbits brought to the island by European ships.

NEVER WAKE A SLEEPING FUR SEAL

One day, while doing research on a remote, volcanic subarctic island named Heard Island, Dana had a close encounter with a grumpy male fur seal, whom she accidentally woke from a nap. Dana stood her ground and shouted as the enormous animal charged, but the seal wasn't deterred and kept coming toward her, snorting and foaming at the mouth. Deciding to run, Dana slipped in an elephant seal wallow and fell into a smelly, slimy depression in the ground. Luckily, this brought her to a lower level than the fur seal. After looking at Dana with a satisfied face, the fur seal rocked back and forth from flipper to flipper as if he were laughing and then returned to his sleeping spot and resumed his nap.

KEEPING ANTARCTICA SAFE

Today, as a senior researcher at the Australian Antarctic Division, Dana is interested in identifying any risks against Antarctic and sub-Antarctic ecosystems and finding ways to keep ecosystems from collapsing in the future. She helped design a biosecurity center at a wharf that serves as Australia's gateway to Antarctica to help keep invasive plant and animal species out.

THE 3As

Dr. Dana Bergstrom works tirelessly to educate the public about the importance of caring for Antarctica. She has identified what she calls the 3As: awareness, anticipation, and action, which are all crucial to conserving the natural world. Dana also used her artistic skills to write a musical called *Antarctica, Beneath the Storm*, which is about a female penguin biologist who travels to Antarctica and experiences the realities of climate change. In 2021, she won the 2021 Eureka Prize for Leadership in Innovation and Science.

HOW SEEDS SPREAD

Use a shoe and a stuffed animal to see how invasive seeds are dispersed.

MATERIALS

- 2 large, flat containers
- Potting soil or dirt
- Chia seeds, wheat grass, or grass seeds not treated with chemicals
- Stuffed animal
- Box to hold the stuffed animal
- Old shoe

SAFETY TIPS AND HINTS

This project can be done outdoors or on a baking sheet to minimize the mess.

PROTOCOL

1 Fill a large, flat container with potting soil or dirt and set it aside.

2 Sprinkle chia seeds into the fur of a stuffed animal. Imagine that the animal is in its natural habit, brushing against plants and picking up seeds in its coat. *Fig. I*

3 Put the animal in a box and imagine it is a rat or cat on a ship traveling to Antarctica. *Fig. 2*

4 Remove the animal from the box and shake it over the container full of dirt to see how it might carry seeds to a new ecosystem and disperse (spread) them. *Fig. 3*

5 Water the soil in the container and keep the soil damp. Check the container every day and see what grows. *Fig. 4*

Fig. 7: Think about how shoes can spread seeds and other living organisms from one place to another.

6 To see how humans can carry seeds on their shoes, in another flat container, mix some potting soil or dirt with water to make mud. Spread the mud on the bottom of a shoe or dip the sole of the shoe in the mud. *Fig. 5*

7 Go outside and sprinkle some seeds on a hard, flat surface. "Walk" the shoe over the seeds as though someone were walking across them. See how many seeds the muddy shoe picked up and think about how shoes spread seeds and other living organisms such as bacteria, viruses, and fungi from one place to another. *Fig. 6*, *Fig. 7*

CREATIVE ENRICHMENT

Let the mud and seeds on the shoe dry. When the mud is dry, walk the shoe over a flat container filled with soil several times, bending it as if there were a foot inside and the person had traveled to another continent or island. Water the "shoe" container to see what grows.

Fig. 1: Sprinkle chia seeds into the fur of a stuffed animal.

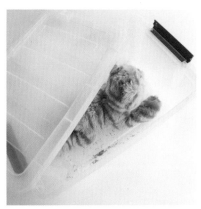

Fig. 2: Put the animal in a box and imagine it is a rat or cat on a ship traveling to Antarctica.

Fig. 3: Remove the animal from the box and shake it over the container full of dirt.

Fig. 4: Keep the soil watered to see what grows.

Fig. 5: Dip the sole of a shoe in mud.

Fig. 6: Sprinkle seeds on a flat surface and walk the shoes over the seeds.

THE SCIENCE BEHIND THE FUN

Seed dispersal is the term used to describe how plant seeds are transported to new places where they can grow and reproduce. Often, animals disperse seeds on their fur and feathers, and in their manure. Humans are also very effective at spreading seeds around the globe, and sometimes they do it unintentionally, by carrying seeds on their shoes and clothing. The introduction of new plant species can be harmful to existing ecosystems, as new plants crowd out native plants by competing for space, sunlight, nutrients, and water.

The introduction of new animals can be harmful as well. Macquarie Island is an example of an ecosystem threatened by new species. Humans hunted the island's penguins nearly to extinction, while rats and rabbits from European ships invaded the island, with no natural predators to stop them. Cats were brought in to control the rats but made things worse. While the cats killed birds, rats ate eggs and chicks. The rabbits destroyed vegetation, eroding nesting areas and causing cliffs to collapse, taking out entire bird colonies. Later, each time the government tried to get rid of one destructive species, the population of another would grow. Finally, in 2014, all the rats, rabbits, and cats were removed from the island.

Aparajita Datta

(b. 1970)

A PASSION FOR BOOKS AND ANIMALS

Aparajita Datta was born in Kolkata, the capital of the Indian state of West Bengal, in 1970. When she was eight, her family moved to Lusaka, Zambia, in southern Africa. Her interest in animals was first inspired by the books of James Herriot and Gerald Durrell and one of her teachers invited her to join the Zoo Club at school. After five years, Aparajita's family returned to India, where she finished high school and studied botany at Presidency University.

THE PAKKE TIGER RESERVE

After graduating from college, Aparajita earned a master's degree from the Wildlife Institute of India. While she was in graduate school, she met Charudutt Mishra, who was also studying wildlife ecology, and they married. In 1995, she went to the Pakke Tiger Reserve in Northeast India to study how logging was affecting wildlife. While she was there, Aparajita became fascinated by hornbill birds and continued to study them for her PhD.

HORNBILLS

Hornbills are beautiful birds with long bills that sometimes look like the horn of a cow. Their beaks are often very colorful and sometimes have a bony protrusion on top. Aparajita's research revealed that hornbills are more than just pretty birds. The birds she studied in the Pakhui Wildlife Sanctuary turned out to be vital participants in the ecosystems they inhabited, spreading the seeds of more than eighty species of trees. In fact, some tree seeds were only spread by hornbills. Aparajita calls hornbills the "farmers of the forest."

SEED DISPERSAL

"Understanding connections and interactions between animals and plants is the part of my work I find most exciting," Aparajita says. "In tropical forests, 80 to 90 percent of tree species bear fruits that animals disperse. But . . . many large mammals and birds like the hornbill—crucial to seed dispersal—are hunted. Some parts of the park have become empty forests, devoid of wildlife. The absence of these dispersers could have severe consequences for the regeneration of many plant species."

PROTECTING HORNBILLS

Aparajita continued to study wildlife in the Arunachal region, which includes the Pakke Tiger Reserve. She did a wildlife census in the area, counting tigers, bears, clouded leopards, and deer in the park. She studied hornbills as well, because they were in grave danger of extinction due to hunting and the cutting down of trees where they nested. Aparajita started to work with the Lisu and Nyishi people in the area, enlisting former hunters to help protect the birds and their nests.

LEARNING FROM THE LISU PEOPLE

Passionate about nurturing people's relationship with the wild, Aparajita set up a nest adoption program. She formed a partnership between people in the cities who offered financial support and people who live in the forest, who protected hornbills. She said, "The Lisu people are right by our side. They've shown and told me things I never would have otherwise known. I think wildlife biologists often forget how much we depend on the insight of local people. To me, part of the wonder of this incredible place is being there with the Lisu, sharing moments in the forest with them." In 2016, the Pakke Tiger Reserve won an India Biodiversity Award for its Hornbill Nest Adoption Program.

IN TODAY'S WORLD

In addition to studying and helping to protect hornbills, Dr. Aparajita Datta is working on projects to restore native tree species to areas where they have been cut down.

NATURAL RELATIONSHIPS

Observe and illustrate the relationships between insects and plants.

MATERIALS

- Magnifying glass
- Camera or device with a camera
- Notebook
- Insect identification app or book
- Plant identification app or book
- Paints, colored pencils, or markers

SAFETY TIPS AND HINTS

Keep your distance from stinging insects such as bees and wasps. Photograph them and zoom in for a closer look.

PROTOCOL

1 Go on an insect hunt. Pack a magnifying glass, something for taking pictures, and a lab notebook. Weed patches, parks, fields, gardens, and wooded areas are good places to look for invertebrates. *Fig. 1*, *Fig. 2*

2 Insects have six legs, while arachnids like spiders and ticks have eight legs. Look for butterflies, bees, wasps, flies, ants, caterpillars, beetles, aphids, grasshoppers, and other insects. Think about the relationship between insects and the plants where you find them. *Fig. 3*, *Fig. 4*

3 Use a magnifying glass to take a closer look at the insects you find. Search for eggs and caterpillars on plants. *Fig. 5*

4 Photograph the insects and the plants that you find them on.

Fig. 5: Use a magnifying glass to look closely at the insects.

5 Record the date, time, weather, and detailed descriptions of what you find in a notebook. Are the insects stationary (still) or moving? Do they appear to be eating plants or collecting nectar? Are they on the stems or leaves of the plant?

6 Print out the photos you took, or draw and paint the insects you photographed on the plants where you found them. *Fig. 6*

7 Use an app or a book to identify and label the insects and plants you photographed. In your notebook, include common and scientific names and the date and location where you found each insect. If you discovered eggs, include those in your drawing as well.

CREATIVE ENRICHMENT

Plant a butterfly garden to provide food and habitat for caterpillars.

Fig. I: Go on an insect hunt.

Fig. 2: Weed patches, parks, fields, gardens, and wooded areas are good places to look for invertebrates.

Fig. 3: Insects have six legs, while arachnids like spiders and ticks have eight legs.

Fig. 4: Think about the relationship between insects and the plants where you find them.

Fig. 6: Print out photos or draw the insects you found on the plants where you found them.

THE SCIENCE BEHIND THE FUN

Every living thing on Earth plays a role in the larger eco-system of the planet, and insects make up an enormous part of animal life. In fact, between 80 and 90 percent of all animals on Earth are insects. They are also the most diverse group of animals on the planet, with an estimated 5.5 million species.

Plants and insects form the foundation of Earth's food web. Most of the plants, animals, humans and other organisms on our planet are completely dependent on insects. They pollinate crops and natural habitats, and many animals, from fish to birds, rely on them as a source of nutrition. Insect populations are on the decline because of habitat loss, climate change, and pesticide use, but it is not too late to help save them.

In this lab, you discovered that many insects depend on plant habitats for food and shelter. By protecting and restoring natural areas and planting native vegetation, it is possible to help insects survive and thrive.

Lisa Schulte Moore

(b. 1971)

A NATURE LOVER

Lisa Schulte Moore grew up in Wisconsin, where she loved camping and visiting her great-grandmother's farm outside of her hometown of Eau Claire. After high school, she attended the University of Wisconsin, Eau Claire to study biology. "From there," she says, "it was kind of just following my interests and passions from one question to another." Her curiosity led her to northern Minnesota, where she did research for a master's degree, studying bird populations affected by wildfires and logging.

BUILDING BRIDGES

Eventually, she completed a PhD in forestry at UW and took a job with the U.S. Forest Service. While she was there, she learned that wildlife biologists and foresters sometimes had problems talking to each other, which makes it harder for everyone to do their jobs of conserving the forest. Realizing the importance of communication, Lisa decided to build bridges between groups who had different goals and priorities, as part of her work going forward.

THE CORN BELT

In 2003, Lisa joined the faculty at Iowa State University, in Ames, Iowa, as a landscape ecologist with a goal of making agriculture work for both people and the planet. Iowa lies in the heart of America's Corn Belt, which was first inhabited by a number of tribes, including Dakota, Ho-Chunk, Ioway, Otoe, Illiniwek, Meskwaki, Omaha, and Sauk. When the U.S. government forced the Indigenous people off the land in the 1800s, most of it was settled as farmland.

RUNOFF

Today, Iowa's farmers produce a large percentage of America's corn, soybeans, hogs, and eggs. Unfortunately, farming can be harmful to the environment. Plowing up prairie to plant crops destroys ecosystems where pollinators, birds, and other animals live. Fertilizer and chemicals that are sprayed on crops to kill insects and stop weeds from growing run off the plants, into the soil, and make their way into the water supply. Lisa understands that while humans need the food, fiber, and fuel produced by agriculture, we must find ways to protect the environment.

PRAIRIE STRIPS

Lisa points out that where corn and soybeans are grown, the fields are bare for most of the year. Without roots holding it down, the soil is vulnerable to erosion by wind and water. Pollution from erosion moves into streams and rivers, ruining the water quality all the way from the Mississippi River to the Gulf of Mexico. Farm fields can also produce greenhouse gases. A prairie strip is an agricultural conservation technique that uses native grasses and plants planted in farm fields to help build soil and clean up rainwater from the fields.

CLEANER WATER, BETTER SOIL

Prairie strips also help keep fertilizer and other chemicals out of streams, rivers, and ponds while providing a habitat for native wildlife. Lisa and her team have shown that by covering 10 percent of a crop field with prairie strips, they can keep 95 percent more of the soil in that field, 77 percent more of the phosphorus, and 70 percent of the nitrogen, so less fertilizer is needed.

HAPPY ECOSYSTEMS

Prairie strips also triple the number of pollinators and double the number of birds. Lisa emphasizes that it is essential for scientists and farmers to work together. Using prairie strips, the land produces more and is damaged less. She hopes that what scientists and farmers in Iowa are learning about using native plants to increase production and decrease environmental damage will someday be used in farms around the world. In 2021, Dr. Lisa Schulte Moore was named a MacArthur Fellow for her work on prairie strips.

PLANT MODELS

Make prairie plant models in a jar.

MATERIALS

- Wide-mouth jar with canning (2-piece) lid
- Pencil
- Brown and blue construction paper
- Scissors
- Chenille sticks (pipe cleaners)

PROTOCOL

1 Remove the flat metal disk from the screw band of the jar lid. With a pencil, trace the lid onto brown construction paper and cut the circle.

2 Use scissors to make a cut from the edge of the circle to the center and cut a small hole in the center of the brown circle. This is where your "prairie plant" will grow. *Fig. I*

3 Look up some images of prairie plants and prairie grasses with long roots.

4 Use pipe cleaners to create a model of a prairie plant. *Fig. 2*

5 Fashion long roots for the plants using pipe cleaners.

6 Twist some worms and root-dwelling insects into the roots.

7 Attach the plant to the roots by twisting pipe cleaners together.

8 Slide the plant and roots into the slot on the paper circle so that it looks like the plant is growing in brown dirt. *Fig. 3*

9 Cut a piece of blue paper to fit into the jar bottom, representing water. Place it in the jar.

10 Put the roots into the jar so that the roots are touching the blue paper and the brown paper covers the jar mouth. Twist the screw band onto the jar to hold the dirt and plant in place. *Fig. 4*

Fig. 4: Put the roots into the jar and twist the screw band on.

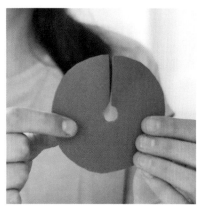

Fig. I: Use scissors to make a cut from the edge of the circle to the center and cut a small hole in the center.

Fig. 2: Use pipe cleaners to create a model of a prairie plant.

Fig. 3: Slide the plant and roots into the slot on the paper circle.

CREATIVE ENRICHMENT

Create a collection of pipe-cleaner prairie plants and grasses in jars.

THE SCIENCE BEHIND THE FUN

Before the Europeans came to the United States, an ocean of tallgrass prairie covered 170 million acres, creating the continent's largest continuous ecosystem. Prior to 1840, around 50 million bison roamed the prairie, which also supported elk, antelope, grizzly bears, panthers, and wolves. Today, corn, soybean, and sorghum fields cover most of the land and tallgrass prairie has been reduced to 4 percent of its original area, making it one of the rarest, most endangered ecosystems in the world, according to the National Park Service.

Prairie plants developed features to help them survive frequent fires, droughts, and fierce competition for nutrients and water. Three-fourths of all the plant material in prairies is made up of roots. The main stems of most prairie plants, called rhizomes (rye-zomes), run horizontally just under the surface of the ground, where they are protected from fire and the elements. Roots extending down from rhizomes to search for water can grow to 15 feet (4.5 m) long.

Lesley de Souza

(b. 1977)

ICHTHYOLOGY

Born in 1977, Lesley de Souza grew up exploring forests and creeks in the southeastern United States and on her family's farm in Brazil. As a child, she loved the outdoors. Lesley and her little brother spent hours on end in forests and creeks, looking for animals. In college, she fell in love with fieldwork, which allowed her to continue exploring streams and rivers. She went on to graduate school and got a PhD in neotropical ichthyology (the study of fish in Central and South America).

THE WORLD'S LUNGS

Lesley's fascination with fish took her to the Amazon Basin and a region called the Guiana Shield in South America, all part of the Amazon rain forest, the largest, most diverse tropical rain forest on Earth. Many people refer to the Amazon as the world's lungs because its trees and plants play an essential role in keeping our atmosphere stable and breathable. The Amazon is a biodiversity hot spot, containing thousands of keystone species, whose populations keep ecosystems healthy.

A RIVER SYSTEM

In addition to collecting fish, tracking their movements, and analyzing their DNA, Lesley pays attention to the bigger ecological picture, including the watersheds. She describes a watershed as a whole river system that is connected to the forest, to the people, and to every aspect of that natural ecosystem. For example, she is interested in the hydrological (water) connections between rivers and lakes that form during the rainy season.

ARAPAIMA

Working with Indigenous people who understand their environment better than anyone else, Lesley studies a fish called arapaima, which can grow up to 10 feet (3 m) long and are strong enough to break your bones if you don't handle them correctly. By installing tiny radio transmitters in the fish, she tracks their movements as they migrate into the flooded forest during the rainy season.

A RAIN FOREST ECOSYSTEM

Lesley says, "There's no way to separate what's happening underwater from the top of the forest canopy. The macaws perched on top of the giant trees are dependent on the fish swimming in the river and vice versa. The river brings nutrients into the soils that are absorbed through the roots and permeate the entire landscape . . . fish feed upon the fruits that fall from the trees."

CONSERVATION FOR THE FUTURE

Like many scientists, Lesley is deeply concerned about ecological destruction in the Amazon. Logging and mining are threatening the fragile ecosystems. Cutting down trees and digging for gold pollutes the air and water, destroys waterways, and demolishes ecosystems so that they can never recover. In addition to studying fish, Lesley is interested in working with the Indigenous people and governments of the places she studies to create conservation areas to ensure a healthy future for the water, the land, and the people who live there.

IN TODAY'S WORLD

Dr. Lesley de Souza understands that it is essential to address environmental issues on a local level, by working closely with governments and people who live in threatened ecosystems. Every ecosystem, no matter how small, plays an important role in the larger ecosystem that is Earth.

ENCLOSED ECOSYSTEM

Build a rain forest terrarium or an aquatic ecosystem.

MATERIALS FOR RAIN FOREST TERRARIUM

- Large jar or small fish tank with a lid
- Pebbles or small rocks
- Activated carbon or charcoal (available online or at pet stores)
- Dried moss
- Potting soil (organic, if possible)
- Tropical plants small enough to fit in the terrarium (such as *Biophytum sensitivum*, *Fittonia*, rock ferns, *Ficus ginseng*, and live mosses)
- Small plastic animals (optional)
- Water
- Spray bottle (optional)
- Plant identification app or book

MATERIALS FOR AQUATIC ECOSYSTEM

Access to a stream, lake, pond, or river (adult supervision required)

Washed and rinsed glass container with sealable lid, such as a mason jar

Gardening trowel, aquarium net, or fine-mesh sieve

Magnifying glass (optional)

SAFETY TIPS AND HINTS

Adult supervision required when collecting by a stream, river, lake, or pond.

Fig. 6: Cover the container with an airtight lid to hold in moisture.

PROTOCOL FOR RAIN FOREST TERRARIUM

1 Cover the bottom of your terrarium container with about 1 inch (2.5 cm) of pebbles.

2 Add a layer of activated carbon to the terrarium. *Fig. 1*

3 Cover the carbon with a layer of dried moss. This will keep most of the dirt out of the rocks at the bottom. *Fig. 2*

4 Put some potting soil on the moss and plant your tropical plants, covering their roots with more potting soil. *Fig. 3*

5 Cover the potting soil with dried moss, live moss, or more small rocks. *Fig. 4*

6 If you want to add plastic jungle animals, put them into the terrarium.

7 Water the terrarium slowly, until you can see a little bit of water in the rocks at the bottom. Spray the plants with water if you have a plant sprayer. *Fig. 5*

8 Put a lid on the terrarium and close it tightly. *Fig. 6*

9 Open the terrarium every week or so to refresh the air inside. If the plants look dry, spritz them with a little bit of fresh water. *Fig. 7*

Fig. 1: Add a layer of rocks and then a layer of charcoal to a clear container.

Fig. 2: Cover the charcoal with a layer of dried moss.

Fig. 3: Add soil to the terrarium and arrange a few small plants in the soil.

Fig. 4: Cover the plants' roots with dirt and then add more pebbles and/or moss.

Fig. 5: Water the terrarium until you can see a little bit of water in the rocks at the bottom.

Fig. 7: When water in the soil evaporates, condensation will form as tiny water droplets inside the terrarium.

project continues ▶

CREATIVE ENRICHMENT

Collect a few shade-loving mosses and small plants from a local yard or wooded area and use them to build a terrarium. Study a plant identification app to confirm the plants are not poisonous before you touch them.

THE SCIENCE BEHIND THE FUN

The ecosystems inside sealed terrariums do not require much water, because they can recycle it. In this lab, you observe the water cycle at work. Energy from sunlight is trapped inside the jar as heat. This causes liquid water in the soil and on the plants to turn to water vapor in a process scientists call "evaporation."

Condensation is the opposite of evaporation. When air is cooled to a certain temperature called the dew point, or it is so full of water vapor that it cannot hold any more, it condenses from gas back into water droplets. Gravity carries the water droplets down to the soil, where plants can drink it. Water trapped inside of a sealed terrarium is constantly recycled—evaporating and condensing to keep plants alive and thriving.

PROTOCOL FOR AQUATIC ECOSYSTEM

1 Find a shallow area near the shore of a stream, pond, lake, or river and use a jar or container to scoop up some water. *Fig. 1*

2 Use a gardening trowel, net, or fine-mesh sieve to scoop up some sand, mud, and muck and add about 1 inch (2.5 cm) of it in the bottom of your jar. *Fig. 2*

3 If you have a net or sieve, try to scoop up some invertebrates such as snails and larvae near rocks and plants. Transfer them to the jar. *Fig. 3*, *Fig. 4*, *Fig. 5*

4 Gather a few leaves, branches, and aquatic plants and add them to your jar. *Fig. 6*

5 Seal the container tightly and put it in a spot where it gets indirect sunlight.

6 If you have a magnifying glass, use it to observe tiny creatures that live in the water. If you don't have a magnifying glass, some of the invertebrates should be large enough to see without magnification. *Fig. 7*

7 Keep the aquatic ecosystem covered tightly so nothing can escape from the container. After a few days, dump it out in the same lake or pond where you collected the water, plants, and animals.

Fig. 1: Fill a container with lake or pond water.

Fig. 2: Scoop up some muck.

Fig. 3: If you have a net or sieve, try to catch some invertebrates.

Fig. 4: Look for movement in the mud.

Fig. 5: You may find clams, snails, and insect larvae.

Fig. 6: Add some aquatic plants from the same spot.

Fig. 7: Observe life in the jar.

CREATIVE ENRICHMENT

Try to identify some of the plants and invertebrates you capture.

THE SCIENCE BEHIND THE FUN

A sealed aquatic ecosystem can also be called a biosphere, because it does not require anything from outside of the jar or container other than sunlight. Plants and algae inside the biosphere use sunlight, carbon dioxide, and water for energy. In the process, they give off oxygen, which is required to keep invertebrates such as snails and insect larvae alive.

Invertebrates eat plant matter and each other, producing carbon dioxide and organic waste. This waste and other decomposing matter are consumed by bacteria and fungi. Nutrients in the sludge at the bottom, along with water and carbon dioxide, are used by the plants to grow. The plants produce more oxygen, and the cycle begins again.

Ayana Elizabeth Johnson

(b. 1980)

A GLASS-BOTTOM BOAT

Ayana Elizabeth Johnson was born in Brooklyn, New York, in 1980 and grew up there. Her mother was a public school teacher, and her dad was an architect. Ayana had always been interested in animals and spent hours digging up worms in her backyard. When she was five, Ayana fell in love with the ocean. Her family had taken a trip to Florida and ventured out in a glass-bottom boat. Staring down through the transparent floor, she was captivated by the magical coral reef below. By the time Ayana was ten, she also wanted to be a lawyer so that she could help people who were fighting for social justice.

BETTER FISH TRAPS

After high school, Ayana pursued her interests in biology and law by studying environmental science and public policy at Harvard University. While pursuing her PhD in marine biology at the University of California's Scripps Institution in San Diego, she traveled to the Caribbean islands of Curacao and Bonaire to do research. Working with local fishermen and divers, she redesigned fish traps to reduce bycatch (Lab 25), which are fish caught by accident.

A COLLABORATION

The collaboration was a success, and the new traps reduced bycatch by around 80 percent, allowing fishermen to catch what they needed while keeping other fish in the coral reef ecosystems safe. Ayana's work on the islands convinced her more than ever that she wanted to take an active role in conservation, rather than writing scientific papers. She then went on to work with the people of the island of Barbuda as they created their own marine regulations.

CHANGE MAKER

In 2016, Ayana moved back to Brooklyn, where she worked with Greenpeace to protect coral reefs and with the World Wildlife Fund. She also started a think tank for coastal cities, called the Ocean Collective, because rising oceans put safety, economies, food security, and communities at risk. In addition to protecting existing ecosystems, she worked on an ocean-centric plan for reducing the amount of carbon we put into the atmosphere and launched a podcast called *How to Save a Planet*.

ENVIRONMENTAL JUSTICE

Ayana points out that environmental protection is a justice issue, saying, "If you think about the rates of asthma in inner-city communities that are near power plants or exposed to other types of pollution, it's a lot higher. And when we think about immigration, and how a lot of migration is now driven by climate change, whether it's droughts and crop failures or the impacts of storms, that becomes a social justice issue that was triggered by the impacts on communities that did the least to emit the carbon to cause the problem." She is passionate about making people aware of environmental justice, because historically marginalized populations are often the hardest hit by the negative impacts of climate change.

RETURNING THE FAVOR

As a science communicator, Ayana likes to point out the role played by the ocean in slowing climate change, which is often overlooked by politicians. She says, "The ocean has already absorbed about 30 percent of the excess CO_2 that we've trapped by burning fossil fuels. And the ocean has already absorbed 93 percent of the heat that we've trapped. And so the ocean is trying its best to buffer us from our worst. We need to return the favor."

IN TODAY'S WORLD

To protect the ocean Dr. Ayana Elizabeth Johnson suggests avoiding plastic containers whenever possible, because plastic waste often ends up polluting the ocean. Keeping your carbon footprint small by walking, biking, using public transportation, and carpooling also reduces the amount of carbon dioxide gas that is soaked up by the ocean.

THE EFFECTS OF CARBON DIOXIDE

Experiment with red cabbage juice to see how carbon dioxide acidifies the ocean.

MATERIALS

- Head of fresh red cabbage
- Pan
- Water
- Strainer
- Large jar or bowl
- 4 clear small jars or glasses
- Spoon
- Baking soda
- White vinegar
- Plain carbonated water
- Rimmed tray or baking sheet
- Small, clear container such as a test tube (optional)
- A paper or reusable straw (optional)

SAFETY TIPS AND HINTS

Cabbage juice is nontoxic, but an adult should supervise the chopping and boiling steps.

PROTOCOL

1 Chop half a head of red cabbage into small pieces and add it to a pan. Cover with water.

2 Boil the cabbage uncovered for about 15 minutes, stirring occasionally. Remove from the heat and let it cool. When the juice is cool, strain it into a jar or bowl. The juice should look purple.

3 Pour some cabbage juice into each of four small cups or jars until they are about half full.

Fig. 5: Baking soda and vinegar react to form carbon dioxide bubbles.

4 To the first cup, add a spoonful of baking soda (sodium bicarbonate). Baking soda is a chemical called a base. Note the color change caused by a base.

5 Pour vinegar (acetic acid) into the second glass of cabbage juice until it is bright pink. *Fig. 1*

6 To the third cup, add tap water or bottled water until it reaches the top of the cup.

7 Add carbonated water (water containing carbon dioxide gas) to the fourth cup until it reaches the top of the cup. Note the color. *Fig. 2*

8 Arrange the cups in order of acidity, from least acidic (blue or green) to most acidic (pink), including the cup with nothing added, which is cabbage juice with tap water. You will probably notice that the cup containing carbonated water is more acidic than the cup containing tap water. *Fig. 3*

9 For fun, do a chemical reaction. Place the glass containing baking soda on a tray and pour the cabbage juice/vinegar mixture into the baking soda to create carbon dioxide gas bubbles. *Fig. 4*, *Fig. 5*

Fig. I: Pour cabbage juice into four cups. Add baking soda (a base) to one and vinegar (an acid) to a second cup.

Fig. 2: The cup containing carbonated water will look pinker (more acidic) because of the carbon dioxide.

Fig. 3: Put the cups in order, according to acidity.

Fig. 4: Combine the pink vinegar cup with the blue baking soda cup.

THE SCIENCE BEHIND THE FUN

Earth's oceans are like giant sponges for carbon dioxide gas. About 30 percent of the carbon dioxide that is released when humans burn fossil fuels and that burns down rain forests is absorbed by our oceans. When carbon dioxide reacts with water, it produces carbonic acid. This results in the ocean water becoming more acidic, like the cabbage juice in this lab when you add carbonated water.

In the two hundred years or so since humans started burning fossil fuels to power factories and transportation, huge amounts of carbon dioxide have entered the atmosphere. As a result of that activity, today's oceans are significantly more acidic. This drop in pH along with other changes in ocean chemistry have made it increasingly hard for certain sea life, including the coral in reef ecosystems, to survive and reproduce.

In this lab, cabbage juice acts as an acid indicator, turning pink or red when acid is added. The carbon dioxide in carbonated water forms carbonic acid. This acid turns the cabbage juice more pink or red than uncarbonated water does.

Jodie Darquea Arteaga

(b. 1980)

A DIVERSE LANDSCAPE

Jodie Darquea Arteaga was born in Ecuador, a country on South America's west coast that sits on both sides of the equator and encompasses the Andean highlands, the Amazon jungle, and the Galápagos Islands. When she was sixteen, Jodie went to study biology at the State University, where her research involved learning to breed and harvest a species of fish called almaco jack.

FROM SHRIMP FARMING TO RESEARCH

While Jodie dreamed of getting a master's degree in marine biology, it was difficult for students who were not from wealthy families to advance in the education system, so she went to work for the shrimp industry. However, she was more interested in conservation than farming shrimp and went to work for Equilibrio Azul, a nonprofit research and conservation organization.

ON-BOARD OBSERVATION

Jodie's new position involved accompanying Ecuadorian fishermen on their boats to observe bycatch in small fishing fleets. Bycatch occurs when nontarget species such as dolphins, birds, and turtles get tangled up in fishing lines and nets. These accidental entanglements often result in the death of the bycatch. Jodie monitored hundreds of these fishing trips, documenting the species and bycatch conditions.

SCRIPPS INSTITUTE OF OCEANOGRAPHY

Jodie also fought hard to protect endangered birds like the waved albatross and worked for the government as chief protector of a marine-protected area called the Pelado. Then, to continue her education, she took two years of intensive English classes and applied to graduate school. Her dream came true when she was accepted to the master's program at the University of California's Scripps Institution of Oceanography. The program was difficult, but she persisted, and in 2016 she received her master's degree in advanced studies in marine biodiversity and conservation.

ECUADOR ECOLOGICAL WORLD

Today, Jodie Darquea Arteaga is an associate research professor at Ecuador's State University of the Santa Elena Peninsula, serving as a mentor to other young biologists. She is part of the team at Ecuador Ecological World, a nonprofit organization dedicated to conservation and the sustainable management of coastal marine resources for the benefit of coastal communities. Jodie and her team do research related to the conservation of ecosystems and threatened marine species in Ecuador. They also promote environmental education, foster relationships with communities, and provide tools to help people manage fisheries, ocean animals, and pollution.

SAVING SEA TURTLES

Before Jodie's work began, there was no documentation of bycatch in Ecuador. Today, alongside other partners, she and her team continue to work with local fishermen. Jodie's latest project provides LEDs (very bright lights) to fishermen to reduce the number of sea turtles that get tangled in their nets. Jodie, who has always worked hard to achieve her dreams, now has a daughter named Maya to accompany her on her expeditions.

IN TODAY'S WORLD

Sustainable fishing reduces bycatch to protect ecosystems and keep fish populations healthy. When buying seafood, look for the blue Marine Stewardship Council (MSC) logo. The MSC is an international organization whose mission is to end overfishing and ensure seafood is caught sustainably.

SAFER FISHING PRACTICES

Go fishing in a bowl to learn about bycatch.

MATERIALS

- Large container
- Plastic sea animals, such as sharks, dolphins, turtles, and fish (or use baby carrots or Swedish fish candy to represent sea animals)
- Floating berries, such as cranberries, to represent fish near the surface
- Produce netting or other net
- Aquarium net or kitchen scoop

SAFETY TIPS AND HINTS

Small children should always be supervised around water.

PROTOCOL

1 Fill a large container with water and add plastic sea animals or Swedish fish. *Fig. I*

2 Put cranberries in the water to represent schools of fish near the surface. *Fig. 2*

3 Use a produce net to try to scoop up the cranberries without catching the plastic animals. Inspect your catch. *Fig. 3*

4 Create a model of a bottom-trawling net using an aquarium net. Choose one fish on the bottom you would like to catch and then pull the net along the bottom, from one end of the container to the other. *Fig. 4*, *Fig. 5*

5 If you don't have a net, use a kitchen scoop to try to catch only one fish. Inspect your catch. Count how many other fish and sea animals you caught by trawling along the bottom and imagine how such a net would damage the ocean floor. *Fig. 6*, *Fig. 7*

Fig. 7: It's easy to see how trawling nets damage the ocean floor and kill marine life.

CREATIVE ENRICHMENT

Engineer a net to catch one species of fish with less risk of bycatch.

Fig. I: Fill a container with water and add plastic sea animals.

Fig. 2: Alternatively, use Swedish fish. Add cranberries to represent fish near the surface.

Fig. 3: Try to scoop out the cranberries with a produce net, avoiding the fish on the bottom.

Fig. 4: Choose one fish to catch and drag a fish net along the bottom, from one end to the other.

Fig. 5: You will probably bring up some bycatch.

Fig. 6: If you don't have a net, use a kitchen scoop to represent a trawling net.

THE SCIENCE BEHIND THE FUN

Thousands of square miles of fishing nets are dragged through Earth's oceans every day. While this is good for the fishing industry, it can be devastating to marine ecosystems and animal populations. Marine life, including turtles, dolphins, sharks, and immature fish, are often tangled in the net, hauled up onto boats, and then thrown back into the water, often dead or dying. These unwanted victims of the fishing industry are known as bycatch.

A method called bottom trawling is especially harmful, as weighted nets are dragged across the seabed, scooping up everything in their path and damaging reefs and habitats. Scientists such as Jodie Darquea Arteaga are working with local fishermen and the fishing industry to help reduce the amount of bycatch. Large organizations such as the NOAA (National Oceanic and Atmospheric Administration) are also working hard to monitor and estimate bycatch.

It's tricky to catch just one type of fish when fishing with a net. To reduce bycatch, it is essential to develop tools that reduce the accidental capture of protected species and unwanted fish. Working with local fishermen and understanding fish behavior are essential to the success of bycatch reduction programs. Today, GPS technology, real-time maps showing schools of protected fish, modified nets, and artificial illumination all show promise as modern bycatch-reduction tools.

ACKNOWLEDGMENTS

I am extremely grateful to all of the talented people who collaborated to make this book.

First, I would like to thank the team at Quarry Books: acquiring editor Jonathan Simcosky, who got me started writing kids' science books; art director Heather Godin; project manager Karen Julian; marketing managers Angela Corpus and Mel Schuit; and the entire design and editing team. I am lucky to have such a skilled, supportive group to work with.

Thank you to my wonderful literary agent, Rhea Lyons.

Special thanks to the scientists who took time from their busy schedules to answer my questions and tell me stories from the field.

Thank you Kelly Anne Dalton for bringing the scientists in these pages to life with your gorgeous illustrations. Thank you to photographer Amber Procaccini for capturing the science projects and kids so beautifully. Thank you, Avery, Cecilia, Claire, Cooper, Divya, Eleanor, Elijah, Gunnar, Haakon, Hadley, Harriet, Henry, Ian, Jackson, Julian, Khloe, Kiran, Lachlan, Madeline, Margaret, Raina, Ravi, Sadie, Silvia, Stella, Sully, and Zach, for being amazing model scientists.

Finally, I'm endlessly grateful to my family and friends, who keep me laughing and learning.

ABOUT THE AUTHOR

Liz Heinecke has loved science since she was old enough to inspect her first butterfly. After working in molecular biology research for ten years and getting her master's degree, Liz left the lab to kick off a new chapter in her life. Soon she found herself sharing her love of science with her three kids, journaling their science adventures on KitchenPantryScientist.com. Her desire to spread her enthusiasm for science to others soon led to regular TV appearances, speaking engagements, and her books: *Kitchen Science Lab for Kids* (Quarry Books), *Outdoor Science Lab for Kids* (Quarry Books), *STEAM Lab for Kids* (Quarry Books), *Star Wars Maker Lab* (DK), *Kitchen Science Lab for Kids: Edible Edition* (Quarry Books), *The Kitchen Pantry Scientist: Chemistry for Kids* (Quarry Books), *The Kitchen Pantry Scientist: Biology for Kids* (Quarry Books), *Sheet Pan Science* (Quarry Books), *The Padawan Cookbook* (Insight Editions), and *RADIANT: The Dancer, The Scientist, and a Friendship Forged in Light*, an adult nonfiction narrative about Marie Curie and Loie Fuller (Grand Central Publishing). Most days, you'll find Liz at home in Minnesota. She graduated from Luther College with a B.A. in art and received her master's degree in bacteriology from the University of Wisconsin, Madison.

ABOUT THE PHOTOGRAPHER

Amber Procaccini is a commercial and editorial photographer based in Minneapolis. She specializes in photographing kids, babies, food, and travel, and her passion for photography almost equals her passion for finding the perfect taco. Amber met Liz while photographing her first book, *Kitchen Science Lab for Kids*, and she knew they'd make a great team when they bonded over cornichons, pate, and brie. When Amber isn't photographing eye-rolling tweens or making cheeseburgers look mouthwatering, she and her husband love to travel and enjoy new adventures together.

ABOUT THE ILLUSTRATOR

Kelly Anne Dalton is an artist, illustrator, and storyteller living in the wild mountains of Montana. Her elegant and enchanting work can be found on everything from board books to middle grade novel covers, home decor and gift products, and stationery lines. When not drawing, daydreaming, and creating new stories and characters, Kelly Anne can be found trail running in the forests near her home.

INDEX